LAS VEGAS
BEHIND THE TABLES!

BARNEY VINSON

GRAND RAPIDS, MICHIGAN

Library of Congress Catalog Card Number: 86-80659

ISBN 0-914839-08-X
(International Standard Book Number)

Photo of author, courtesy of Lee Phelps.
Photo of craps table, courtesy of the Desert Inn, Las Vegas, NV.

Contents

The author wishes to express his appreciation to those who consented to interviews for this work, including:

Hank Greenspun, Publisher of the Las Vegas Sun

Sonny King, Las Vegas entertainer

Bob Brooker, General Manager, Marina Hotel

Earl Junker, Dice Supervisor, Dunes Hotel

Robert Harrington, former Casino Manager,
Tropicana Hotel

Tony Foley, Assistant Cage Manager, Caesars Palace

Dick Maurice, Las Vegas columnist

Bill Borland, World-Wide Casino Exchange, Las Vegas

Mort Saiger, Executive Casino Host, Frontier Hotel

Eddie Church, Supervisor, Dunes Hotel

Roger Mennie, Corporate Security, Dunes Hotel

Paul Burst, Executive Vice-President,
Claridge Hotel/Casino, Atlantic City

With special thanks to
John Gollehon, James Thurman and Debra Phillips.

For Debbie, My Girl Friday,
and Saturday and Sunday
and Monday . . .

INTRODUCTION

The Indians called it "The Meadows." Mormon pioneers settled there, a little over a hundred years ago. Out of this desolation rose the most exciting city ever built; in fact, the fastest-growing U.S. city of the twentieth century.

How did this man-made resort come to be? Whose idea was it? Why do a million people a month come to this place, this Disneylandish oasis in the desert?

Is it the excitement of big-name stars and Parisian reviews, the 24-hour action, the two-dollar buffets? Or is it the lure of Lady Luck, that outside chance of winning a fortune, facing the gods head on in battle and coming away the victor. Or does it really matter, deep inside, whether you win or lose?

Nicholas Dandalos perhaps said it best. Better known as Nick the Greek, he put it this way, "The most exciting thing is to win. The next most exciting thing . . . is to lose."

It was during this country's biggest depression that gambling was introduced in Nevada, and the hard-earned dollars rolled in. One oldtimer said, "It was like a beautiful

1

flower growing through a crack in the sidewalk.'' Or was it a beautiful weed?

Today those dollars are still rolling in. Gaming revenue in 1984 in Clark County alone (which *is* Las Vegas) was $2,007,902,677. Another *three billion* dollars went into the local economy!

Gambling brought it all about; the game of chance; the idea of getting something for nothing; easy money. Some say even God himself gambled, when he created Man in the first place.

In Greek mythology it is said that Mercury, in love with the earth and wanting to give her more light, gambled with the moon and won five extra days of moonlight.

The first records of gambling are Chinese, around 2300 B.C. Gambling flourished in ancient Greece, even though it was against the law. The emperors of Rome—Augustus, Claudius, Nero—were avid gamblers. Loaded dice were discovered in the ruins of Pompeii, crafted from the knuckle bones of goats and sheep.

The Old Testament contains references to the drawing of lots to determine God's will, which had direct bearing on the tossing of Jonah into the sea and the division of ancient Israel among twelve tribes. Later on, Roman soldiers gambled for the garments of crucifixion victims. "Pythius, I'll let you have this robe I won for two pieces of silver. Then I'll have enough to take Bethsheba to the gladiator matches.''

One of the most famous gamblers of all time had to be Christopher Columbus. For, if certain 15th-century theories on the shape of the world had proved correct, he and his crew would have fallen right off the edge of the earth, never making it to this continent.

There is also a legend that the Spanish sailors on Columbus' ships whiled away their time at sea by playing cards. Deciding that the cards were bringing them ill luck and that they were sailing to their doom, they threw them overboard and promptly sighted land. On shore they got bored again and made a crude deck of cards from the leaves of the copas tree. If there is any truth to this tale then the first playing cards in America were manufactured in 1492.

Then there was the Earl of Sandwich (1718-1792), who loved to gamble so much that he had his cook bring him his favorite meats and cheeses between hunks of bread when he was at the tables. And these weren't dinner tables, either. From that came the popular word "sandwich."

Cowboys gambled a month's pay on a turn of the cards in the wild west. Next to the jail and the general store the saloon and gambling hall was the most popular place in town. In Las Vegas it still is.

So it's the nature of the beast. People will wager a bet on practically anything, from a high school football game to a Presidential election, and anything in between. How about those million-dollar sweepstakes that come in the mail from magazine clearing houses? Putting it bluntly, you're gambling the price of a stamp that you're going to win a fortune.

Insurance? Anyone who buys insurance, whether it's from an agent or even from one of those quarter-machines at an airport terminal, is betting his life against a certain amount of money that he *is* going to die. It's a bet that he certainly doesn't want to win!

When you get right down to it you'll have to agree that there is not one person reading this right now who hasn't gambled at one thing or another in his lifetime.

Want to bet?

CHAPTER 1

In The Beginning

Out in the middle of nowhere, circled by a ring of mountains in a sandy barren valley, lies America's most glittering jewel. The little sign you see on your way into town from the airport says it all. "Welcome to Fabulous Las Vegas!" (Another sign leaving the city says just about as much: "Free Aspirin and Tender Sympathy.")

But Las Vegas isn't where we begin our book. The back sections of New Orleans were where gambling first mushroomed in this country. It wasn't exactly *legal*, but no one seemed to mind. There was also organized gambling in Florida, Kentucky, and Ohio, spreading throughout the South and Northeast, up until the 1940's.

One of the biggest casinos of this pre-war era was the Club Devon in Toledo, Ohio, which got most of its business from Detroit, 50 miles away. It was equipped with 23 craps tables, 35 blackjack games, and had 45 ticket-writers in its horse-racing parlor. The main reason it didn't have to worry about being raided by authorities was because the owner was the local sheriff!

Then came Nevada Assembly Bill Number 98, in 1931, which lifted all gambling restrictions (except lotteries) in Nevada.

In the same week that legalized gambling in Nevada was okayed by Governor Fred Balzar the new six-weeks divorce law was enacted. That meant that not only could people come to Nevada to lose their money . . . they could lose their *mates* at the same time.

Of course, all of this didn't spell the end of illegal gambling in other parts of the country.

"New Orleans operated just like Vegas," remembers Dunes executive Earl Junker, who worked as a dice dealer in Louisiana during the early forties. "You could walk into a sports book or into a dice game right off the sidewalk."

These "back games," as they were called, tried to stress *class* all the way. Not only did the dealers wear jackets, and in some cases tuxedos, but necktie and coat were usually required for all male customers.

Of course, if a player had enough money and planned to gamble until it was all gone he could have probably gained entry to any casino anywhere, even if he were dressed as a cigar store Indian! Take the case of Big Fist Magoo. He was built like a lumberjack, never shaved, weighed at least 250 pounds, and had hands the size of manhole covers. One night in an illegal club back East, Big Fist Magoo was at one of the tables when three armed men burst in. Before escaping with the bankroll they ordered all the men in the club to drop their pants. To everyone's surprise, Big Fist Magoo was wearing pink ladies' bloomers!

A well-known Las Vegas pit boss, now deceased, loved to fish but he couldn't swim. So he would tie himself to the mast of his boat while his boat was tied to the dock. The only thing he liked better than fishing was gambling. In fact, it was said that the reason he came to Las Vegas in the first place was because he kept losing all his money in St. Louis gambling houses. His friends took up a collection to send him and his family to Vegas, but he never made it with the money. He stopped just once on the way, and that was at a notorious "bust-out joint" (crooked casino) on the outskirts of St. Louis. "How could you do that?" his friends cried. "You knew that place was a flat store!" He shrugged and said sadly, "It was the only game there was."

Bust-out joints, flat stores or flat-bed stores, phony balonies . . . all two-bit words that meant the same thing: Gambler, beware! Crooked casinos would mark the cards, slip in loaded dice, rig the roulette wheel, anything to increase the profits even more. Most had specialists, or "gaffers," on their payroll who were called in when their services were needed . . . just like the family doctor.

There was a Florida casino in the late forties that practiced its own version of "The Sting." Every person in the club, except maybe one unsuspecting gambler, would be on the payroll . . . dressed to portray senators, doctors, actresses. "It was like a goddamned movie set," remembers the oldtimer who told this story. "And when the *real* gambler left the casino, minus his money, everyone was paid, and the costumes were put away, until the next high-roller came to town."

A dice dealer once auditioned for a job in an early Las Vegas casino after having worked at a number of illegal gambling houses in the South. He was doing great until the shooter rolled a winner four, and then the dealer just stood there. "Pay everybody," the boss told him. But the dealer replied, "I don't know how. Nobody ever made a four at the places where *I* worked."

Earl Junker, talking about a Louisiana casino that was open during the war, said, "They had stickmen (on the dice table) who actually had callouses on their hands from holding a pair of dice along with the stick. Now, when a shooter came up and got a point . . . say he rolled an eight . . . the stickman would let him roll two or three times if he was making come bets. And then the stickman would bring the dice back to the center of the table and reach out to put some propositions up, and pick up the good dice and drop the balonies and let 'em go.''

"A lot of times crude joints would let the guy get a point and whack him out the next roll. No, they'd give him two or three rolls to get a little more money and *then* whack him out!"

A dealer who worked at one of the first casinos at Lake Tahoe in northern Nevada remembers one of the club's favorite ploys. "If a guy was watching the craps game, and I could tell he knew how to play, I'd drop a couple of black checks (hundred-dollar chips) on the four and kind of look around like I was making sure no one else was watching. Then I'd give him a wink and say, 'Do you want odds on your four?' And he'd pick up on it immediately and come out of his pocket with two hundred in cash. Those dice would bounce down the table like a couple of flat tires . . . loser seven. I'd give the player a shrug as if to say 'sorry' and we'd have another two hundred in the can.''

A gaming veteran who dealt craps in an Ohio casino before World War II says, "I remember when we worked on the graveyard shift, and we'd get down to one or two players on one end of the table. Well, if one of the dice got behind the money rack it was an automatic loser, no matter what happened.'' Then, with a laugh, he added, "We had this Greek, he would shoot the dice from one end and run all the way down to the other end before the dice even stopped. He used to say, 'You no call-a me out, you son-a-bitch. You no need a stick-a-man with me.' "

More reflections. "I was working with a guy, he was busting (cheating) from the stick . . . and we had red and green dice in those days. Well, the player was shooting red dice, so the stickman came in with the phonies, and they were *green*! I thought we were all going to get *killed*, but nobody noticed! And the joint was loaded!"

Most of the players must have been loaded, too.

Other ways of cheating the customers included shorting them on various pay-offs, and removing a goodly portion of face cards from the blackjack decks. According to the man who tells these stories, who has been in the business almost 50 years, these "gaffs" were even used in some Las Vegas casinos up to the mid-fifties.

"At the blackjack tables, a high roller would come in, the boss would pick up the phone and call a certain dealer from the dealers' room, 'Come on down,' and he'd do his duty.

"Or some guy at the dice tables would have a thousand on the four and a thousand on the ten, and the next roll there wouldn't be nothing there. And they'd tell the player, 'You ain't got nothing, sir. That was *last* hand.' "

And on and on. "This strip hotel had five or six dealers, I'm not going to mention their names, these guys are working today. A certain high roller would walk in, you'd go to that table. You'd work an hour, you'd crack him out, go on a break, the next guy would crack him out, you'd follow him. That poor guy never had a chance. I'm talking big money, seventy, eighty, a hundred thousand at a whip. In those days."

Of course, it would help matters if the player was under the influence of alcoholic beverages while all this was going on. To expedite that procedure as quickly as possible the casino would "special" their drinks. They did this by adding a shot of vodka to whatever drink the player was having, be it a Brandy Alexander or a plain glass of beer. If the player became obnoxious once he was broke, his next drink would be his last. It seems a healthy shot of vodka, subtly blended with a healthy shot of Visine, tends to make a healthy person head straight for the bathroom as fast as he can.

In 1955, the Gaming Control Board stepped into the picture in Nevada, and the days of shaved dice and skinned customers ended, more or less. This board was created from within the Nevada Tax Commission, which had been overseeing legalized gambling since 1946. Before that, it was all under the control of the county Sheriff's departments.

It should be stressed, however, that not all casinos—even the illegal ones—employed such underhanded practices. They didn't have to. As "luck" would have it, and mathematical probability, the odds are well in the house's favor in all casino games. The more customers a casino draws the more money the casino will make. But the green-eyed devil called Greed still lurks in the hearts of men. "I got to tell you," says one Las Vegas pit boss, "if it wasn't for all the surveillance, if it wasn't for those high-technology cameras they got everywhere, and if it wasn't for the Gaming Control Board, we'd *still* be ripping and tearing."

Indeed, former Nevada assemblyman Phil Tobin—who introduced the Nevada gambling law in 1931—commented in later years, "If the control board hadn't ultimately been created, we wouldn't have gambling today."

Early Las Vegas

If the clock were turned back just a little over a hundred

years ago, to the year 1881, Las Vegas was nothing but sand, cactus and a few bubbling waterholes. An Ohio farmer by the fanciful name of Octavius D. Gass owned much of it: 800 acres that was to eventually become downtown Las Vegas. Gass owed a fellow named Archibald Stewart six thousand bucks, six thousand which he didn't have. But he had the land, so he gave *that* to Stewart.

Stewart had the property only one year before he was shot dead by a drunken ranchhand. His wife and sons farmed it until 1902 and then she sold it for $55,000 to Montana Senator William Clark. Clark wanted the land for his railroad. Those bubbling waterholes turned out to be natural underground springs, and water was a necessity if Clark were to fulfill his dream of building a railroad connecting the Pacific Ocean with the Great Salt Lake.

Clark's line was called the San Pedro, Los Angeles, Salt Lake Railroad Company . . . later to become part of the Union Pacific. In those days the steam locomotive needed water . . . water which Clark found in Las Vegas.

The railroad needed something else, too. It needed a town. So in 1905 Clark cut his land up into townsite lots. It was a gamble, just like everything else, but Clark booked one of the biggest winners of the times. He sold each lot for $500 at auction and wound up with over a quarter of a million dollars, plus some degree of immortality when the county in which Las Vegas nestled was named after him.

Nevada had already gained some degree of importance as a state, not because there was anything there but because it was right in between California and the rest of the country. People who wanted to go to California—people like American soldiers and gold miners—had to go through

Nevada to get either east or west. Behind them they left mining camps, churches, cemeteries, and saloons.

The saloons offered the miners plenty of watered-down whiskey and plenty of gambling. It had all been legal in Nevada since the 1850's and was a way of life there. Even before the arrival of the white man, native Indians played their own gambling games. The losers were probably the ones who had to attack the wagon trains.

Then came this ominous headline in the San Francisco Examiner on October 11, 1910. "Legalized Gambling Has Drawn Its Last Breath In The United States." The Nevada Legislature had finally bowed to public pressure and ordered all gaming establishments to close their swinging doors, and suddenly it was a felony to operate a gambling game.

In the following years the law was relaxed a bit. Social games were permitted, as long as they were played only for drinks and cigars, or other prizes under two dollars in value. After that came the new "nickel-in-the-slot" machines, but none of this appealed to red-blooded American gamblers. It was almost like playing bingo in the church basement.

The operators of these games and machines weren't happy either. They had to be licensed by the local government and they had to pay annual license fees to run their clubs. So everyone started going "undercover" and that made the state unhappy because nobody was paying their license fees.

In 1931, the 35th session of the Nevada Legislature decided that a change was again necessary. In that year the so-called "wide-open" gambling bill was passed.

While all this was going on, six giant contractors were busy insuring Las Vegas' future as a unique American metropolis. They were spending almost $50 million build-ing Hoover Dam some 30 miles away. This 726-foot high dam, dedicated by President Roosevelt in 1935 after four years of construction, tamed the mighty Colorado River. More important, it provided Las Vegas with enough water, through Lake Mead, to satisfy its needs to the turn of the century and beyond.

Nevertheless, even with legalized gambling, even with Hoover Dam right down the road, nothing much was hap-pening in Las Vegas. There were a few small casinos on Fre-mont Street downtown, such as the Boulder Club, the Apache Hotel (later to become the Horseshoe Club), the Pioneer, the Monte Carlo, and the Las Vegas Club.

Upstate it was a different story. Reno, Nevada, which billed itself as "the biggest little city in the world," was where the action was. Reno had a lot going for it. . . snowcapped mountains, picturesque lakes, furry pine trees; it was close to the state capital and close to California. It had Harold's Club, which blanketed the United States with billboards proclaiming "Harold's Club or Bust," and broke gaming out of its cloak of secrecy. It had William Harrah's Tango Club, and it had Warren Nelson, who introduced keno to the state in 1936.

Over at Elko, Nevada, there was the Commercial Club, which pioneered the use of big name entertainers to attract business. For the price of a drink, unheard of before, you could see Ted Lewis and his band, Sophie Tucker, Paul Whiteman, the Dorsey Brothers, Lawrence Welk, and the Andrews Sisters.

So the logical question is *why did Las Vegas become the gambling capital of the state*? It's one of the hottest places in the country; temperatures sometimes climb to 120° in summer. People there say it's like living on an island with a minimum of five hours driving time to get anywhere else. When it rains, which it hardly ever does (4.13 inches a year), the water crashes through town sweeping away trees, houses and in some instances people. So why would anyone in their right mind spend millions of dollars building a gambling casino in Las Vegas? Especially when all the successful gaming operations were up in the other end of the state.

The official word is that with the construction of Hoover Dam "it was believed that the dam itself would become a major tourist attraction, encouraging a thriving resort hotel trade."

The *unofficial* word is a little different. One high-ranking casino executive, who wouldn't allow his name to be used, is still deserving of the following quote because it makes a lot more sense than the preceding paragraph:

"Originally, the 'boys' who wanted to open up Nevada went to Reno. They wanted to open up Reno. But they were turned down; the city fathers wouldn't allow them. So they came down here, to Las Vegas. Reno would have been perfect, nice weather, the four seasons."

It was much easier to get a gambling license in Las Vegas before the Gaming Control Board came along in 1955, and the hotels started going up like building blocks:

1940	El Rancho Vegas
1943	The Last Frontier, Nevada Biltmore, El Cortez
1946	The Golden Nugget, the Flamingo
1947	The Thunderbird
1950	The Desert Inn
1952	The Sahara
1953	The Sands
1954	The Riviera

1955   The Dunes
1956   The Hacienda
1957   The Tropicana, the Mint
1958   The Stardust
1963   The Castaways
1966   The Aladdin, the Four Queens,
         Caesars Palace
1967   The Frontier Hotel
1968   Circus Circus
1969   Landmark, Las Vegas Hilton

Each new resort brought new customers to Las Vegas, and additional fame to the city.

One of the men who made it all happen was a handsome young thug named Bugsy.

Bugsy Siegel

In the early days of gambling in Nevada there was no doubt in anyone's mind that there were going to be problems later on. Robbins Cahill, former Secretary of the Nevada Tax Commission, said, "You didn't get bishops of the church and solid upright outstanding citizens who were in the social register that wanted to go into the gambling business. They were people who were gamblers. And because Nevada was the only state where it was allowed legally they, of course, had to get their experience in states where it was *illegal*."

In 1941 they came, they saw, they conquered. The first of this new breed of "businessmen" was a short Jewish guy named Moe Sedway. It turned out that he was a trusted disciple of racketeer Benjamin "Bugsy" Siegel, and Sedway's job was to set up the Trans-America wire service in

Nevada. This wire service, controlled by the Al Capone mob in Chicago, was the bread-and-butter of Vegas bookmakers handling horse races. Without it they could all be past-posted (betting *after* the race is finished) into immediate bankruptcy.

The bookmakers' bread-and-butter soon turned to bread-and-water. Bugsy himself was in Las Vegas by 1942 and—with no arguments from anyone—started helping himself to as much as two-thirds of the income from the casinos' bookmaking operations. He also managed to acquire an interest in the Golden Nugget and the Frontier later on.

According to the book "The Green Felt Jungle," Siegel then went back to California, leaving his good friend Gus Greenbaum to oversee things. But Bugsy had a dream. "He would build the largest and most luxurious gambling casino in the world, one that would not only be a casino and a hotel but a nightclub with restaurants, bars, exotically landscaped grounds and the finest service imaginable." It would make Bugsy legitimate, so legitimate that "no FBI man can ever as much as lay a finger on my shoulder."

When he was thinking about building his hotel, Bugsy told his cronies, "We're gonna give this place a real first-class name. We'll call it the Flamenco." "How come?" his friends asked. "You know, after them gorgeous pink birds that stand around with one foot up in the air." Ralph Pearl swears this is a true story, in his book "Las Vegas Is My Beat."

The early forties had already seen tentative steps in the direction which ultimately would become the Las Vegas Strip. The El Rancho Vegas had opened three miles south of town on the Los Angeles highway. It wasn't an overwhelming success but it pointed the way for things to come.

Next came the Last Frontier, a little farther out on the highway, with the slogan "The Early West In Modern Splendor."

Thus the trend was started. But it was Siegel's hotel which finally drew national attention to Las Vegas.

Bugsy called his hotel The Flamingo, later changing the name to The Fabulous Flamingo. It was supposed to cost $1.5 million to build, but that skyrocketed to $6 million before the hotel opened on December 26, 1946. And that six million included all of Siegel's "stash" plus a little under $5 million from his racket pals.

Incidentally, a rumor persists to this day that Bugsy built a secret room in the Flamingo, when the hotel was being constructed, and inside that hidden place still lay hundreds of thousands of dollars in cash!

June 20, 1947.

Allen Smiley, an acquaintance of Siegel, was visiting with him in Beverly Hills that night. "Ben (Bugsy) had just settled down on the sofa to read the paper when all of a sudden there was a hell of a racket, shots and everything. When I looked up at Siegel I could see he had taken most of them."

Gus Greenbaum was next. He had been in charge of the Flamingo for Siegel and later headed the Riviera. But it seems he was taking more out of the till than his paycheck.

About this same time, Wilbur Clark started building the Desert Inn, but ran into financial difficulties and borrowed enough money to finish the hotel in 1950 from Cleveland's Moe Dalitz. When the smoke cleared, Dalitz and his associates owned 74 percent of the Desert Inn . . . and Wilbur Clark was left in the dark, with *six* percent.

In a few short months, Senator Estes Kefauver called for a hearing on organized crime in Las Vegas. The 1951 hearings resulted in a black eye for Vegas ("Exaggerated," cry local papers) and the creation of the State Gaming Control Board.

To this day, Las Vegas has never been able to rid itself of its reputation as a mob holding.

A floorman at the Mint Hotel remembers when he overheard a cocky young tourist tell his wide-eyed girl companion, "These places are all run by the Mafia. They take all the money off the top and send it back to Italy." So the floorman walked over to the whispering couple and said in his gruffest voice, "Scuse me, youse guys care for a drink or nuttin'?" "No, thank you, SIR," they both screamed, and then—as the floorman walked away—the young man mumbled to his girlfriend, "See what I mean?"

Howard Hughes

It was apparent that Las Vegas needed a hero, a Captain America to give Nevada some class. And in 1966 here he came.

Hank Greenspun, publisher of the Las Vegas Sun newspaper, knew Howard Hughes just about as well as anybody ever did. Greenspun remembers driving with Hughes and Del Webb through the Las Vegas desert. Webb would later open the Sahara and Mint hotels.

"We were in this little Chevrolet, and it was hotter than hell. And Webb said, 'Howard, open up the damn windows, we're gonna *suffocate.*' Hughes said, 'I can't, because I'm allergic to the dust.' And Webb said, 'Howard, I don't give a shit. I don't want to die in this god-damned car!'

"And Hughes said, 'You know, I've got a perfect way to overcome this allergy that I have and still live in Las Vegas. I would take thirty acres, put it under glass, air-condition it, and build a home right in the middle of it. It would be germproof.' That's the way the man used to think.''

Howard Hughes was many things to many people. To Hank Greenspun he was a savior. Said Greenspun, "There's no question that his advent into gaming was a tremendous plus in this respect: it opened up avenues of financing that were closed before, institutions like banks . . . insurance companies . . . Wall Street. Can you imagine some woman back then who was a shareholder in Fireman's Fund in Boston appreciating Fireman's Fund investing in gambling? It would have rocked Boston!''

Greenspun said he was in his attorney's office in Washington when a call came from Robert Maheu. "He was a trouble-shooter for Hughes. He had never *seen* Howard Hughes, but he was a former FBI agent, and he was employed to make things 'compatible' for Hughes . . . keeping reporters away, that sort of thing.'' Hughes was staying on the fifth floor of a hotel in Boston, and the news reporters were getting desperate. They had even pulled the fire alarm, and when the firemen rushed to the fifth floor the reporters were right behind them. Maheu was complaining about all this to the attorney, who was an old friend of his, and said that Hughes was thinking of moving to an island in the Caribbean so he could get a little peace and quiet.

Greenspun finishes the story. "So Ed Morgan (the attorney) turns around and says to me, 'It looks like Howard Hughes might be going to the Caribbean.' I said, 'Why doesn't he come to Las Vegas? He always loved it here. At least, there's more excitement in Las Vegas. We could hide him away, you know, and he could still have the excitement.' And Morgan says, 'That's a good idea.' And he called Maheu back.''

Maheu, who always referred to his unseen boss as "The Man," agreed to a Las Vegas move, providing two floors could be reserved at a top Vegas hotel. The original thought was to put Hughes in the Dunes, since it was the tallest building in town at the time. When that didn't pan out "we were able to procure the two top floors of the Desert Inn." That's the way it all came about, said Greenspun, "despite what you read, despite what the rest of them say."

In November of 1966, Howard Hughes and his staff of Mormon yes-men made a midnight exodus into the regal penthouse of the Desert Inn. To Hughes it was like coming home, because—as Greenspun said—"some of the most pleasant times Hughes ever had were spent in Las Vegas, going back to the late forties. In fact, he had little places around where he kept girls stashed away. He did the same thing in Los Angeles at the Beverly Hills Hotel, and at the Wilshire, although he'd never enjoy them. It's known as meaningless proprietorship."

A month goes by, and Desert Inn owner Moe Dalitz is getting fidgety. New Year's is coming up, and Dalitz has no place to put his holiday high rollers. He gives Hughes orders to vacate the premises, and once again Greenspun found himself in the middle of history. This was the scenario:

Las Vegas was trying to clean up its act. Moe Dalitz was considered by some people to be an unsavory character, but he was a *rich* unsavory character who owned the Desert Inn and the Stardust, and he was trying to get his hands on the Riviera. Greenspun was using his newspaper to campaign against this multiple-ownership of Vegas casinos by Dalitz and his partners, "because I didn't want an extension of their influence." The two meet face-to-face, in a modern-day version of the gunfight at the OK Corral:

DALITZ: I want Hughes out of here. I need those rooms for New Year's Eve.

GREENSPUN: Howard Hughes has big plans for Las Vegas. I don't think it's in your best interest to put him out.

DALITZ: Well, why don't he buy the damn place?

GREENSPUN: He might.

DALITZ: Well, if we sell him the Desert Inn can we keep the Stardust?

Greenspun called Ed Morgan. Ed Morgan called Robert Maheu. Maheu sent a note to Howard Hughes. Eventually a price is agreed on. Thirteen-point-two million. Greenspun bannered his "scoop" in the Las Vegas Sun. "HUGHES BUYS DESERT INN." Maheu called Morgan. Morgan called Greenspun.

"You just killed everything," Greenspun was told. It seemed the deal had hit a snag. Howard Hughes found a $10,000 discrepancy going back to 1954, and he wanted the sale price on the Desert Inn lowered by that amount. "Here the guy's a billionaire," Greenspun laughed, "but that's the way he was. He loved to deal."

Howard Hughes wasn't that hard a person to figure out. He loved to bargain, he had the megabucks to do it with, and he loved his privacy. He hated reporters, because they invaded that privacy. And he hated to pay taxes. Who doesn't? He had lost Trans-World Airlines in a big legal battle, winding up with $529 million; he had over half a billion dollars in the bank, with the interest on that money running to $87,000 a day. If he didn't reinvest that money he would have had to give most of it to Uncle Sam.

What to do, what to do?

The press made him out to be some kind of weirdo,

sneaking around the world with his entourage. A scandal sheet offered $5,000 to anyone taking a photograph of the poor guy. He was rumored to have hair down to his knees, and toenails half a foot long. He owned the Desert Inn, but he still had more money than he knew what to do with. He had to spend it, or lose it. So?

So he bought Las Vegas. Or as much of it as he could get away with. The Sands, the Castaways, the Frontier, the Silver Slipper, the Landmark. And not just hotels, but mining claims, all over the state. Then:

"Howard Hughes owns or holds options to buy nearly every plot of raw land on both sides of the Strip from McCarran Airport to the Sahara Hotel, a distance of some four miles." (Los Angeles Times)

Land! That's where the money was, not on the gambling tables. In the mid-forties, when the war ended, an acre of sand on the Las Vegas Strip could be had for around $5,000. The Summa Corporation, which owns all that land now, won't say what it's worth. A conservative guess by Las Vegas realtor Rob Scott is well over a million dollars an acre, which would break down to over $4,807.69 a front foot.

All told, Howard Hughes spent nearly $300 million in the state of Nevada during this mid-sixties buying spree, making him the state's largest employer and the holder of more licenses than anyone in its history.

It was around that time that Howard Hughes sent the following memo to his aide, Bob Maheu:

"I like to think of Las Vegas in terms of a well-dressed man in a dinner jacket, and a beautifully-jeweled and furred female getting out of an expensive car—I think that is what the public expects here—to rub shoulders with VIP's and stars, etc.—possibly dressed in sport clothes, but if so, at least good sport clothes. I don't think we should permit this place to degrade into a freak, or amusement-park category, like Coney Island.''

Then the jokes started. If a reporter couldn't get an exclusive story on what Hughes was going to buy next, or where he was going to go next, or what he was going to do next, then how about some funny stories?

"Did you hear the news? Howard Hughes bought the Review-Journal Newspaper.'' "How much did he pay for it?" "A dime, just like everyone else.''

"Did you hear the news? Howard Hughes almost got killed this morning. He was walking across Lake Mead and got hit by a speed boat.''

"Did you hear the news? They're changing the name of Las Vegas. They're going to call it Hugheston.''

"Did you hear the news? Howard Hughes got his wife a set of clubs for Christmas. The Sands, the Frontier, the Castaways . . .''

Did you hear the news? And the people laughed, a little nervously, but they laughed. They were afraid of Howard Hughes because of all they had read in the newspapers and all they had heard on the TV. They didn't understand him, and no one ever saw him. In Las Vegas, people weren't even sure there *was* a Howard Hughes. All they had was the word of a bunch of Mormons who were supposedly living with him in the top of some hotel, and that didn't make sense either. Maybe he was dead, and the whole thing was some kind of Communist conspiracy. It made people uneasy, because almost a third of the state's work force toiled in the casinos and they had no idea what was going to happen to their jobs or their future.

Did you hear the news? Howard Hughes was gone! Just like that. He had moved *into* the Desert Inn in the middle of the night. He moved *out* of the Desert Inn in the middle of the night. His next stop was the Bahamas, and then Mexico. On April 5, 1976, in a plane trying to get back to Texas where it all started, he died.

Frontier Hotel host Mort Saiger knew Howard Hughes when both were young men. He said that even then the man was a genius, that his mind was always working. Saiger reflected about the Howard Hughes he knew, and there was a faraway look in his eye.

"I met him here in '44. I was a single fellow then, and my room was right below his in the Frontier. He used to come in from the lake every afternoon, where he was building something. Wearing blue jeans or overalls, and sneakers. No tie. Really not dressed like the man he was, more like a common laborer.

"But he was always polite. And nice. And he used to say to me, 'Mort, what are you doing tonight? When do you get off?' I told him, 'I'll be off at seven.' He says, 'We're going over to the El Rancho for dinner. I want you to join me.' Now I felt so honored. Here I am, just a working individual. There's a man, a millionaire even then, befriending me.

"We went out several times together. He liked to talk to me about Poland, where I was from. And, of course, we ate and enjoyed ourselves. One other remarkable thing, he never had a dime in his pocket. I always paid the bill. But there was a fellow here by the name of Bill Gay who worked for him. [Gay would later run the Desert Inn.] And Howard Hughes would say, 'Tell Bill how much you spent, and he will give it back to you.'

"And so it was."

Just about everyone agrees that Howard Hughes was good for Las Vegas, and that there were two periods of growth in the area's existence: Before Hughes and After Hughes. But it wasn't all roses.

"He took the intimacy out of the casinos," said one observer. "The personality of the whole gambling business has changed. There's a lot of jealousy in this town now. They see a guy's on the ball, and he's doing a good job, and he's getting recognized by a lot of people— they get rid of him."

Another gaming boss from the early Hughes days brought out an interesting point. "In the old days, before Hughes, if you got fired from a job you just walked across the street and got another one. Well, Hughes bought six hotels, so then if you got fired in one of his hotels you automatically couldn't get work in five more, because he owned them all, and he wasn't going to fire you in one and hire you in another. And then, too, he had all these guys working for him, and after a while they were spread out all over town. So you were liable to get canned anywhere, just because of somebody who used to work for somebody who used to work for Hughes."

The years of Howard Hughes are gone, but his mark was forever felt in Las Vegas. In fact, his Summa Corporation still owns those six hotels.*

Altogether, 14 publicly-owned conglomerates moved into Nevada during the late 60's and 70's, gobbling up 25 major casinos and spitting out about half the total gaming revenue for the state. The days of Bugsy and his boys never happened, or happened so long ago it was nearly forgotten. Las Vegas was "almost" clean. As one onlooker

*The Nevada Legislature, in 1967 and 1969, passed several acts which forever changed Las Vegas. In simple terms, these acts permitted publicly-traded corporations to be registered as holders of gaming licenses. This was done to provide a broader base for investment in the gambling industry and in the hope of giving Nevada that long-sought respectability.

said, "The corporations are so big and powerful they don't need the mob; they don't *want* the mob; hell, they could eat the mob for dessert!"

Indeed, Howard Hughes and the advent of corporations gave Las Vegas that long-sought respectability. Millionaire Kirk Kerkorian added to it when he built the International, now the Las Vegas Hilton, and later the huge MGM Grand Hotel. Steve Wynn took over the Golden Nugget in downtown Las Vegas and spent $60 million transposing it into one of the most glamorous resort hotels in the world.

According to Bob Brooker, Executive Vice-President of the Marina Hotel, the corporations today give the player something too. "In the old days of organized crime, people thought there was a lot of cheating going on. Today, people are more relaxed. They know that the large corporations are running everything. And they trust them."

The big corporations may have given Las Vegas "respectability" and "trust," but they also gave it something else. Something it *didn't* want.

Concerned mostly with making money, these new corporations did an about-face from what had always been the informal, "down-home," casino policy. There were three new words for every department: profit, profit, profit. Dealers who smiled and helped players with their bets were "hustling," and job security—which had never been all that stable anyway—became more and more of a problem. Gamblers started to feel they were being greeted and treated impersonally, as entries in a space-age machine and not as individuals.

Casino veterans resented that they were being forced from the foreground and referred to the modern age of the corporation as "the new school of bankruptcy." Surprisingly, many of today's casino vice-presidents and others in the upper echelon have never worked on the front lines in the casino. They've never been in the trenches.

Bob Brooker sums it all up nicely. "Most of the old-timers, who have been here for years, don't like changes. And they don't understand the new image of the corporation, that each department should either make money or at least try to break even. In the old days people just didn't care, they felt that the casinos could carry the operating costs of all the departments. But it just doesn't happen that way."

Indeed, the whole aura of gambling has changed. Suddenly the word "gamble" is passé. The new corporations don't like to use that word. It has a sinister sound to it, an old-fashioned ring that conjures up images better forgotten . . . images of speakeasies, loaded dice, and wayward husbands coughing up the rent money while sobbing wives wring their handkerchiefs and comfort their ill-clothed children.

The new word is *gaming*.

CHAPTER 2

The Dealer

There are still a few glamour jobs left in this work-a-day world. Jet pilot. Actor. Ball player. The guide on the Jungle Cruise at Disneyland. Fashion model. President of the United States. Las Vegas dealer.

The picture that comes to mind when you think of a Vegas dealer is somebody in a starchy shirt wearing gold rings and gold chains, flipping out cards and raking in the money. Dealers are assumed to drive flashy cars and live at the top of a chrome high-rise.

But what is it *really* like, behind the tables?

"It's just a job," one dealer said at a taping session for this book. "After a while the glamour wears off. And . . . it's just a job, like anything else."

"I don't believe that," another dealer disagreed. "Because if I go to any other job, there's no chance that I'm going to have to deal with as many different personalities under stressful situations in one day. If I go to work somewhere else and a guy comes up and starts hollering at me . . . hey, there's only one of them. And one guy hollering, that's nothing!"

The other dealers are starting to loosen up now.

"A lot of people come here from small towns, and before

28

they even get here they've already decided, 'Well, I don't know anybody in Las Vegas, I'm going to be an animal.' And they are. They live up to every letter of the word."

"They think we all live in the hotel. They think we all have maids. They think we get chauffeured to work—"

"And we're all rich!"

"People don't know anything but the Strip and downtown. They don't know that we have schools here, and hospitals, and parks."

A woman dealer: "People think we're all for sale. That there's no normalcy to any of us. Well, we're just normal regular people who grew up in the towns they're coming from . . . and came here to try to make a living."

"And they'll say, 'What kind of guy *is* Frank Sinatra? How many stars have you seen?' I've been living here six years. Who have I seen? I haven't seen anybody."

Being a dealer in Las Vegas *is* a crazy way to make a living. The fancy word for it is "croupier," but if you ever called a dealer that he would probably look at you and say, "Whaat? It's dealer, buddy."

Becoming a dealer requires a period of apprenticeship, like any other trade or profession. First, he will usually go to one of the half-dozen dealer's schools scattered around the city. Unless his uncle owns the Four Queens, or something.

The Las Vegas phone book has all these schools listed in the yellow pages. There's the Strip Dealers School, the International Dealer's Schools (two locations), the Casino Dealers School, the Lady Luck Dealers School, Las Vegas Valley School of Dealing, Nevada Gaming School, Nevada School of Dealing. Day and evening classes are offered, plus job placement "assistance," even government grants and loans.

Job placement assistance means the school tells you where to go, and when you get there the casino boss tells you where to go.

These specialized schools will teach you how to deal a casino game, and you will pay (and pay) to learn that game. It costs anywhere from $500 on up to learn how to deal craps, blackjack, poker, roulette or baccarat. Some of the schools are telling students they must learn three different games, in order to get a job. Cost? Twenty-two hundred. And it's just simply not true. If a person knows one game, and he can deal that game proficiently, he can get a job— providing he knocks on enough doors, and his appearance is halfway presentable.

Each of these schools crank out an average of five dealers a week. That doesn't sound like much until the number of graduating dealers is multiplied by the number of dealer's schools around. For the sake of argument, let's stick with a figure of half a dozen schools. Six times five is 30. That means 30 fresh young recruits are marching into the fifty-odd Las Vegas casinos each and every week, their diplomas in their hands . . . or almost 1,600 a year . . . all after the jobs of those already in there. It's worse than trying to keep a job with a professional football team.

Then the U.S. government got into the act. The Civil Rights Act, that is. In 1963 the government said "there shall be no discrimination against sex." In 1964 the government said "there shall be no discrimination against national origin or race."

The casinos didn't seem to get the message. After all, there were black porters and Chinese laundry-workers, and there were plenty of girls hustling cocktails and running Keno tickets. But then came something called the Tellas Consent Decree, in 1981. That's when the U.S. Equal Opportunity Employment Commission filed a discrimination suit against the unions and approximately 20 Las Vegas hotels. Now it's a whole new ball of wax. Each casino must have a certain number of female dealers, Oriental dealers, and black dealers. If they don't, they get fined. End of story. White adult males who are still holding on to their dealing jobs refer to themselves as "dinosaurs," the last of a dying breed. Because where are *they* going to go? The U.S. government didn't say anything about *them* getting jobs hustling cocktails and running Keno tickets.

Meanwhile, the dealer's schools keep advertising in the yellow pages . . . and they keep pumping out replacement "parts," five a week, every week, just like clockwork.

So why would anyone in their right mind want to be a dealer in the first place? It's an expensive job to learn, and hard to land a good job once you've "graduated." It's near minimum wage, and most inexperienced dealers have to start downtown at the smaller casinos. Some don't even begin as dealers; they're hired either as student dealers or as shills. A shill is a casino employee who acts like he's gambling, in order to entice others to the table. Breaking in, that's what they call it, and it's tough.

Years ago these student dealers seldom even *saw* the tables. They parked cars, cleaned rooms, or ran errands. The money was rotten, the food was rotten and the working conditions were rotten; being a real bonafide dealer in some of these places wasn't much better. One sawdust joint gave its help free soft drinks at the lunch counter until some player hit a Keno ticket for $1500. Then the employees had to start paying for their drinks.

Let's hear from the dealers again.

"I worked for a guy one time . . . he called the pit boss from Florida and said, 'How are we doing?' The pit boss said, 'It's hard to hear you.' He said, 'Yeah, I'm in the car. So *how are we doing*?' The pit boss said, 'We're stuck. One table's losing ten thousand.' The owner said, 'Fire the crew.' Just like that.''

"I think the reason this business has a lot of stress is because people are trying to have control over something that's purely chance. And that's what it all comes down to. They're trying so hard to control something that you can't have control over. It's killing them. And they pass it right on down.''

"If you run a basic game your p.c. (house percentage) is going to hold up. But what happens to most of these joints is that they screw with the games so much. This guy says shuffle now . . . this guy says don't shuffle now . . . cut the deck here, cut the deck there . . . surrender for half your bet in one place, no surrender in another place. You don't know what the hell you're doing! Leave the damn cards alone and the p.c. will be there.''

Working conditions?

"When I worked day shift, they would expect you to come in every Saturday at 11 a.m. and work until 1 a.m. the next day. Fourteen hours, every Saturday. And if you didn't do it, if you called in sick or anything, it was automatic termination.''

"Oh yes, you're expected to do it, with no questions asked.''

"The worst thing of it all is what they do where I work. They'll leave you on a table without even telling you you're working overtime. Like your life is nothing, and it doesn't matter if your husband is out in the parking lot waiting for you at four o'clock in the morning.''

"I believe that the major problem in the gambling

business is the lack of any kind of stress test for executives—"

"How about a competency test?"

"They lose their sense of humor—"

"I think it's because it's the first responsible job these kind of people have ever had. You put them out in the real world and they would never be over anyone. I mean, they're mental morons!"

But the dealers hang in there. Most of them are in the racket for one reason, and it's spelled dough-re-mi. Wages vary from casino to casino, but it's anywhere from minimum wage, even on the Strip, to a high of around $40 (per 8-hour shift) at a few select places. The dealers aren't really that concerned about their pay scale. They usually don't even get a paycheck after declaring their tips every two weeks.

Tips! That's the name of the tune. For some reason, unbeknownst to man, dealers have their own secret little vocabulary. Tips are referred to as "tokes." Possibly because they call chips "checks," and checks—or chips—used to be called tokens.

A few dealers bungled into the business by accident. They might have been in between jobs, looking for something different, the victim of a busted wheel bearing and unable to get out of town, or divorced, or just broke. Then, wandering through a casino with all those chandeliers and the smell of riches everywhere, they see the dealers with their patent-leather shoes and patent-leather hair styles, oozing money . . . making more in one night than somebody else could make in a whole week. How do you get a job like that?

Bingo. The dealer's schools scoop up another student, one sixteen-hundredth of a year's output. And he learns all those secret little words, too. Tokes, checks. George. That's somebody who bets for the dealers. Super George, or King Kong. Somebody who bet a *lot* for the dealers. Stiff. Someone who doesn't bet for the dealers. Super Stiff? Forget it, this guy doesn't even pay his *bills*.

A "duke" is a big hand on the table. "Paint" is a face card. A "snapper" is a blackjack. "Skinny Dugan" is a loser seven at craps. A "barberpole" is a stack of chips, or checks, that are all mixed up, every color in the rainbow.

Some of the others you've heard before. "Boxcars" is a twelve at the dice table, and aces are "snake-eyes." Once, during a hot and heavy hand in Vegas, a woman threw a chip to the stickman. Wanting everyone to know how sharp she was at the game, she screamed, "Gimme a dollar on *snake lips*!"

Here's another true story. Joe Bernstein was a famous gambler, along the lines of Nick the Greek. He would always gather a crowd around the tables because of his big bets and equally-famous short temper. One time at a dice game, he bet $2,000 against the point of four, laid another $4,000 against the four, and overlaid another $4,000 against the four. Here came the dice on a hard four, or two deuces, and Bernstein was suddenly out ten grand. "Winner four!" the stickman called, looking into the angry eyes of Bernstein, "and he made it with a toodly two." "A *toodly two*?" roared the gambler. Then, unable to control his anger, he dropped to the floor . . . crawled under the table . . . and bit the stickman in the—on the—lower posterior. Guess you might say the stickman became the "butt" of a very popular Las Vegas tale.

Las Vegas dealers dream of that big score, the super jackpot, enough money to make up for all the lean times, all the abuse, the cigar smoke, and the overtime. Enough cash to leave Las Vegas in the rear-view mirror. But the big score never seems to come.

The tape is rolling.

"I've been in this business since 1969, and the biggest score I ever made was sixteen hundred."

"Two hundred and twenty-five was mine."

"Four hundred."

"Seven ninety-six."

"Thirty-six hundred."

"We made seventeen hundred one night."

Thirty-six hundred? That's a lot of loot for eight hours work, but it should be pointed out that big paydays like that are few and far between. Dice dealers have a better shot than anyone else of really getting lucky. Baccarat used to be "the" job for dealers until every place in town opened a baccarat pit. Roulette dealers and blackjack dealers pool their tips, and that makes a big score even more unlikely. But now a majority of Vegas casinos are forcing their dice dealers to pool tips, too. "It's not fair, it's not right; the money belongs to the dealers and the casinos shouldn't have anything to do with it." But who's going to stop them? It's a known fact that when dealers have to share their money with everyone else they're not going to hustle as much, because they're only getting maybe three cents out of every dollar that goes in the box. Consequently, the chances now of finding more than one picture of Ben Franklin in a dealer's "toke" envelope are about as rare as a pit boss's smile.

Atlantic City can take some of the blame for what's happening to dealers. Eastern casinos not only put all the dealers' gratuities into one big pot, but then all the deductions are taken out of the money right then. The dealers wind up with two paychecks . . . one with their hourly wages; the other with their tips, less local tax and state tax and federal tax. It makes the whole job rather—taxing.

The forecast is that the same thing will eventually happen in Las Vegas, and any other area of the country that might someday have legalized gambling.

And who loves it, baby? The Internal Revenue Service! Before New Jersey got gambling in 1978 the IRS generally didn't bother the dealers in Nevada too much. A dealer was expected to declare *something*, but if he could show that he lived within his income he really wasn't hassled. After all, there were inequalities on both sides. The dealers weren't declaring all their tips; some weren't declaring *any* tips. (Visiting hours are 3 to 5 on weekends.) Dealers who *were* declaring their tips weren't getting the benefits that other American wage-earners were getting. Tips weren't included in unemployment compensation, on-the-job injuries, that sort of thing. So the argument from the dealers was, "They're not taking care of me. Why should I take care of them?"

Then Atlantic City opened, and the dealers were making money. The IRS knew the dealers were making money, because it was all right there in black and white. The dealers in Nevada were all of a sudden under scrutiny. Something was rotten in Denmark. Or in Nevada, anyway. So the IRS did something it had never done before. If the dealers in Las Vegas, and elsewhere in the state, would start "playing fair" and declaring all their tips, they wouldn't be questioned about any year preceding 1981 . . . which was when this amnesty deal was offered. All that the dealers had to do was keep monthly calendars on their tips and affix their signatures to the amnesty paper. Just sign on the dotted line and it was smooth sailing ahead.

"I complied," one dealer said. "They sent me these calendars with a note to call them and they would explain everything. I called the IRS office, and—I swear to you—this lady told me, 'Where it says *name* you put your name. Where it says *address* you put your address.' I said, 'wait a minute. Do you think you're talking to a total idiot?' "

"I complied," another dealer said. "And I'm being audited anyway, because some dealers declared more tokes than I did. But they worked more than I did."

The IRS over-reacted, one dealer said. "They completely over-reacted. They assumed that when a dealer signed the amnesty he was a thief. Otherwise, why would he sign it?"

The IRS attached the paychecks of one dealer for declaring his tips and *not* signing the amnesty, while another dealer . . . who had never even sent in a tax return for fifteen years . . . got off the hook because she said she didn't know you had to. One dealer, working in a casino on the brink of bankruptcy, had his payroll check attached by the government, and—when his check bounced—the IRS fined *him*. Talk about adding insult to injury.

But the dealers didn't fight the IRS, or fight the casinos when their own money was being taken away from them, and divvied up with everyone else in the place. *Bosses* even started cutting themselves in, in the baccarat pit. The dealers didn't fight when—one by one—their co-workers went out the door for mysterious reasons like:

"Reduction In Staff"

A dealer, who had been working in the same casino for 15 years, could be walking out to the time office after eight hot hours on the table, talking and laughing with guys he'd known half his working life, and get that long low look from the timekeeper. And a slip of paper. With these words on it:

"Change In Personnel"

This doesn't happen to cocktail waitresses. They have a union. It doesn't happen to restaurant waiters, busboys, and cooks. They have a union. It doesn't happen to change girls, stagehands, and musicians. They have a union.

The dealers don't. There have been a few attempts over the years to organize the dealers, but nothing has really materialized. At the Frontier Hotel, the dealers and the Teamsters Union have a contract "under negotiations," but the rest of the dealers in town will probably never be able to sing "Someone To Watch Over Me." If someone in management even hears the word "union," a whole new batch of termination slips will start flying, and they'll all say the same thing: "reduction in staff," "change in personnel."

The money is still good, or the dealers wouldn't be there. A top dealing job is worth about $30,000 a year (including tips), on the average. Enough perhaps to put up with the stress and the tension, the back pain and the neck pain, the lack of any kind of retirement plan or pension plan. A customer once asked a dealer if there was any type of profit-sharing program in the casinos. And the dealer said, "Yes. As long as you don't get caught."

But job insecurity is the big numero uno.

A dice stickman was fired in one Vegas casino for smiling when he called a "winner six the hard way." Another dealer was fired for not answering the phone on his day off, and one was terminated for having a funny message on his answer machine. A dealer, stickman, and a boxman were all fired at one hotel because the dealer accidentally overpaid a player by *two dollars*, and nobody saw it. Among the three of them, they had over 40 years experience in the gambling business. One dealer got the ax for wishing a player a Merry Christmas. Being sick, especially on a holiday, is just asking for trouble. Maybe instead of the dealer wishing the player good luck, the player should wish the dealer good luck.

The hotels pass out rule books and procedure manuals to its employees, and dealers hope that by following these guidelines they will last through another winter . . . make it through one more cut . . . and for once in their life buy something on time like everyone else in America.

"DEALERS SHOULD TRY TO AVOID USING THE WORD 'LOSER.' " So they don't say that dirty adjective on the dice table. It's "seven out, winner on the don't."

"NEVER DISPLAY EMOTION WHILE DEALING." Okay, it's head low and rear end high, and as little conversation with the player as necessary.

"MALE EMPLOYEES ARE NOT TO HAVE BEARDS OR MOUSTACHES." (And they say there's no discrimination in this country any more.)

The Caesars Palace manual for dealers had this to say about courtesy. "Dealers spend more time with the casino customers than any other employees. It is imperative that the dealers let the customers know Caesars appreciates their business. This generates and promotes growth, stability, job security, and monetary rewards for everyone."

That is true. The visitors who come to these gambling meccas do so with the intention of spending their money, of practically giving it away. The whole time they're in town they are face to face with the cab drivers, tour guides, bellhops, registration clerks . . . and the dealers.

So what happens? The hotels treat these front-line soldiers like peons, and—human nature being what it is—this attitude is passed right on down to the customer. "How come you people never smile?" the customer will ask. And a dealer, who has just been called a cuss word because the house lost a bet, or who has just seen a friend fired for some absurd reason, will give him a surly stare as if to say, "Drop dead, mac."

Who can blame him? Look at the Grand Hotel, that cloud-probing neon landmark that squats on the busiest corner of the Las Vegas Strip. It first opened for business in 1973, barely a dozen years ago, with some 4,000 employees. Since that time, over 45,000 workers have gone in the front door and out the back. Forty-five *thousand*! Almost the total population of Las Vegas in 1950, not just the city but the whole county.

Job turnover doesn't just affect dealers. How many times have you read where even the president of a large casino has "stepped down to pursue other interests." Baloney. He got *fired*. That's what happened.

In the old days, if a dealer was looking for a job, he went into the casino and saw the shift boss. If there was an opening he auditioned, and he either got the job or he didn't. When civil rights was just a baby, a black dealer once approached the boss in a Vegas casino and said he wanted to audition. The boss shifted the cigar in his mouth and muttered, "So what do you do—sing or dance?"

Times have changed. Now a dealer first goes to the personnel office and fills out a lengthy employment application. Then there is a thorough security check. If he gets through that he might have to take a lie detector test. This is "to screen out dishonest workers and apprehend those who have committed crimes."

The Marina Hotel first began using lie detector tests in 1984. "We had a major problem in the slot department. We knew someone was stealing, because the percentage we were holding was just too low." This is Bob Brooker talking, who is in charge of casino operations there. He decided to give everyone in the slot department a lie detector test. "And when we started, we found that their answers were deceptive, that they were stealing money. Ever since then we've given lie detector tests on a pre-employment basis. And I'd say that about twenty-five percent of the people can't pass them."

Not only are lie detectors used before employees are hired, they are sometimes used *after* employees are hired . . . as random tests to determine that all is still fine in Eden.

"One of the things you have to learn in this business," said Brooker, "is don't trust anybody. Your employee today who is a good solid employee may start running around, or having some financial problems, or start taking dope. And your good employee is no longer good. You can't trust him."

Granted, maybe lie detector tests do work. Sometimes. Ronald Reagan thinks so. He signed National Security Decision Directive 84, which made it okay for the government to adopt the use of "aperiodic, non-lifestyle counter-intelligence-type polygraph examinations." Secretary of State George Shultz got so mad he almost quit.

Courts almost uniformly refuse to admit lie detector test results as evidence of guilt or innocence. Congressman Jack Kemp of New York says, "It is time we extend the same basic protection to workers which we offer hardened criminals." The 13.2 million-member AFL-CIO says abuse of these devices is "rampant," that at least 50,000 workers a year in the U.S. are wrongfully denied employment because of refusal to take the exams or because of inaccuracies in the testing.

Some people allege to know all the ins and outs of beating this gumball gadget, of maybe curling their toes around a nail or some other metal object and throwing the machine off. Some people say that works, or taking a dozen aspirin right before they strap the wires on you. "Huh? What'd you say? I must have dozed off."

The Elko, Nevada, Daily Free Press expounded on forced lie detector testing. "Each person earns for himself a reputation as a result of the way he conducts his life. Although there are exceptions, the reliability . . . loyalty . . . and honesty of an individual can be forecast best by his past actions, which is to say his reputation."

All this time the dealers have been talking in the other room. Let's listen in.

"When I first started in this business I loved it. I absolutely loved it. I couldn't wait to go to work. I was at the Silver City, and it was small enough for everyone to enjoy each other's company. We got along . . . everyone told jokes . . . we had a good time. And then, as the places get bigger and bigger, it's like—"

"Like working in a factory."

"Right."

"Well, that what it was like when I broke in at the El Cortez. I mean, we were like one happy family. After work we'd all go to the back bar, and play a few poker machines. It was fun."

"I had a totally different experience breaking in at the El Cortez. This was in 1979, and I was the only female in the dice pit. It was brutal. You'd have the same players coming in every day, and they *hated* women! They'd say, 'Why don't you go bake a cake.' Finally, one day I had had all I could take, and this old man said to me, 'Why don't you go bake a cake.' I said, 'Why don't *you* go bake a f---ing cake!!'"

"This town changes your whole vocabulary."

"Sure. You go home and you're embarrassed to talk to your family."

"I hated this job from Day One. My neck hurt, from having my head down all day. I was dealing to a bunch of crudballs. The only good thing about it was I made seventy dollars in one day, whereas it took me *two* days to make seventy dollars in San Diego."

"I saw a guy die on the table once. He's on the floor; the rescue squad is there. The shift boss jumps over the ropes and gets the guy's credit card. 'The son-of-a-bitch owes *fifteen thousand*,' he says. His checks were still on the table, and the shift boss told me, 'count out fifteen thousand, kid.' "

"Cold."

"We had this dealer named Chico, and he was dealing twenty-one to this real sore-head. He tells Chico, 'If you make a twenty-one just one more time I'm coming over this table after you.' Chico called the floorman over. 'This guy just threatened me.' The floorman said, 'Deal him out, Chico.' The player glared at the floorman and said, 'Maybe I should come over the table after *you*.' The floorman said 'Deal him in, Chico.' "

A survey by sociology professor James Frey, which took almost two years to complete, brought out some interesting statistics about casino dealers. The survey revealed that 80 percent of the dealers interviewed would rather be working outside the gaming industry, and that 68 percent didn't see themselves in this business five years from now. Seventy percent of the dealers in the survey said they did not like dealing as a living, and a like percentage of dealers found their jobs uninteresting. For all the unpleasant aspects of the job, Frey noted that casinos are still besieged by more dealers than there are jobs. His survey indicated that most dealers are in it for the short term, with 86 percent saying that they never know when they might get fired.

CHAPTER 3

Surveillance

Ever wonder why dealers clap their hands before leaving the tables? No, it isn't because they're so darned *happy* to be getting out of there, although maybe that's part of it.

It's all in the Dealer's Rules and Procedures booklet. "Clap, spread hands and fingers, and turn toward the supervisor with palms showing." In other words, the dealer is saying to his boss, "See? I didn't steal anything. Not even one lousy chip."

The same goes for tucking in shirts and adjusting ties. Dealers don't do it, not unless they want "The Eye In The Sky" calling down on them. Eye in the sky? That's a two-way mirror that runs the full length of the casino ceiling. In the old days there were surveillance people on the other side of that glass . . . monitoring the action, the players, and the dealers.

A new Las Vegas resident once overheard someone mention this "eye in the sky," and thought for a minute he was talking about a conversation he had held with *God*.

Not quite.

Nobody really calls it "the eye in the sky" any more. With the passage of time it has been abbreviated, just like everything else in Las Vegas. People call it "the eye" now. Las Vegans shorten the names of things for some reason. Las Vegas is Vegas. The Desert Inn is the DI. The Tropicana becomes the Trop, the Riviera the Riv, and the Showboat is "The Boat." A blackjack dealer is in "Bee Jay." And see if you can figure this one out. "I work grave on the wheel at the Shoe." Translation: "I am employed on the graveyard shift as a dealer at the roulette game in the Horseshoe Club."

The "eye" is quite a bit different from days of yore, back when there were a series of narrow catwalks in the ceiling above the mirrors. In those days a dealer could always tell when somebody was tromping around up there. Suddenly dust would start to filter down, and occasionally a piece of ceiling plaster. And everyone *knew*. "The Eye" was watching.

"It was very, very unsophisticated," recalls Dunes security man Roger Mennie. "When I first came to work here nine years ago we didn't have this new surveillance system. We had the old catwalk. And you had to go all the way outside the building, go around by the restaurant, climb up two rickety ladders, just to get inside. You're bending down, stepping over rafters, cobwebs getting in your face all the time. And it was dark. You couldn't have any bright lights because they would show through the one-way mirror."

Unsophisticated is hardly the word for it. Sounds more like a scene from Edgar Allen Poe's "The Premature Burial."

The crowd in one Las Vegas casino was treated to a rare sight once, during these days, when there was the sound of glass shattering and—sure enough—up in the ceiling was a man's leg dangling helplessly through what was left of a one-way mirror.

"We had a guy fall through the one at the Hilton," Mennie recalled. "He was walking to the eye, and he slipped and fell into one of the convention areas."

In 1973 these surveillance men (or what was left of them) breathed a sigh of relief. Suddenly it was "lights—camera—action." Television had come to the rescue. Today each hotel has a number of video cameras, concealed inside large, black plastic, bubble-like fixtures suspended from the ceiling. These remote-control cameras can scan every square foot inside a casino. The technology is so sophisticated that they can zoom in on a penny and let you read the word "liberty." In the major resorts, these video systems are manned 24 hours a day.

These electronic marvels cost anywhere from $250,000 up to a whopping $1 million, and that's just black-and-white. For living color it's another million. As Tropicana surveillance manager Les Weidenfeld says, "they pay for themselves almost immediately, just in the deterrent effect. It keeps honest people honest." As for catching a thief, that's just icing on the cake.

The whole idea of inside snooping has changed over the years. At first it was all hush-hush. Roger Mennie:

"I remember when I first went into the business. The first time I was in the eye in the sky was when I worked at the Hilton. And you weren't allowed to let anyone know who you were. You went through a door that nobody else used, and you went out that door. You didn't eat with the regular employees; you ate by yourself. And the only one who knew you were up there was the casino manager. A few places are still like that, but most of them aren't."

The Tropicana *wants* people to know how it is protecting the customer's assets, and the hotel's. Says Les Weidenfeld, "We have the most sophisticated surveillance system on the Strip. Fifty-one different cameras connect to 16 TV monitors and tape recorders at two stations on the casino's second floor."

Thirty-one of those cameras, housed in their plexiglass bubbles, are suspended along the 4,250 foot stained glass ceiling that domes the Tropicana casino. Operated by controls at the monitoring stations, these cameras—with their pan and tilt functions—systematically train on all gaming tables in the hotel. They can move 365° horizontally, and 175° vertically . . . with focus, iris and zoom controls. The other 20 cameras used by the Tropicana are all stationary. They are trained on the progressive slot machines; the counting rooms; and the cage, where cashiers buy and sell chips, cash checks and take care of markers.

The people who monitor these cameras are taught what to look for in a 480-hour training program, the only one of its kind in Las Vegas. Demonstrations of crooked moves are given by representatives from the State Gaming Control Enforcement Commission and by ex-cheaters, or "crossroaders," as they are known in gambling jargon.

These shady characters usually fall into certain categories:

Claim Bet Artist

He generally works around dice tables, where players often lose track of their bets on the complex greenery. He's good at what he does, and most of the time he gets away with it. If he stops a game to argue most casinos will pay him off, just to get the dice in the air again.

Hand Mucker

He conceals cards in his clothing or hands, and switches them with the ones he's dealt. He's a firm believer in that axiom "the hand is quicker than the eye." And he's never heard that other one . . . "crime does not pay."

Dauber

Remember finger painting when you were a kid? Well, the dauber learned how to make money at it. He dots certain cards with a bit of paint off his finger, cards he will recognize later. Sometimes ultraviolet paint and special sunglasses are used.

Bender and Crimper

A bender puts a very slight bend on the corners of cards he wants to remember. A crimper does just what the name implies; he slightly crimps different areas of special cards. Hand muckers, daubers, benders, crimpers . . . four good reasons why cards are mostly dealt *face-up* nowadays on Las Vegas blackjack tables. The player is not allowed to touch the cards.

Slugger

He is one of the many who prey on innocent little slot machines. Authorities estimate that up to $20 million is lost annually, just in Clark County, to slot machine cheats. The slugger, who uses slugs instead of real coins, is one of the most blatant. Roger Mennie said, "I caught a guy slugging a machine once. I said to him 'Do you know what you're doing is against the law?' 'What do you mean?' he says. 'There was a guy outside the hotel selling these dollar coins for fifty cents a piece. I figured it was a good deal so I came in and started playing them.' I called the Gaming Control Board, and they didn't go for his story, either."

Stringer

He may not know all the ropes, but he can pull a few strings. These strings, or fishing wire mostly, are attached to the coin through a small hole. The stringer will "yo-yo" the coin until it triggers the coin-acceptance switch of the slot machine. He will usually be surrounded by several partners who are called "blockers." Their job is to block his efforts from the view of surveillance agents.

Magnet

He concentrates on the older slot machines. He places his trusty magnet on the side of the machine, which stops the clock and lets the reels float free. When a jackpot is "lined up" he pulls away the magnet and—presto!

Believe it or not, slot machines generate 50 percent of a casino's profit, so slot cheats are a force to be reckoned with. One ring, based in southern California, literally terrorized nine Las Vegas hotels—including the Las Vegas Hilton, Stardust, Golden Nugget and Flamingo—before being apprehended in 1985. Ring members would "win" jackpots by using access keys, special electronic tools, and rigged "PC board" parts that would reprogram the machine's on-board computer. Now, most machines will alert a central computer operator when it is being opened, even when access is required for routine service by the casino. It would seem as if the more sophisticated slot machines have only resulted in more "sophisticated" thieves.

The latest chapter in this never-ending, ever-escalating war is the use of foreign coins, ones that resemble American money but worth only a fraction as much. One man, charged with using these, had 10,000 of them in his car . . . but he had already dropped 90,000 in the slots!

Said Stan Romanski of the State Gaming Control Board, "We can't estimate the loss of gaming revenues each year from the illegal use (of these coins). However, every time such coins are run through a machine and a jackpot is hit, it's almost a free return on the investment."

Will Rogers once said that "what this country needs is a good five-cent cigar." What Las Vegas needs is a tamper-proof slot machine. Rumors abound that one is on its way, but Bob Brooker of the Marina doesn't think that day will ever come. "There will never be a tamper-proof machine. By the time a new computerized slot machine comes out, the cheater has one in his house and he's already examining it. I know of instances where slot cheaters are actually sending people to *college* to get engineering degrees . . . so that when new electronic equipment comes out they can dissect them and learn how they operate."

Sometimes fate plays a mean trick on these culprits. During a strike several years ago by the Culinary Union against the Vegas hotels, picketers kept pulling the electrical plug on the neon marquee in front of the Marina. Brooker and his assistants ran outside to turn the lights on again "and as we were walking back we saw this panel truck in the parking lot. The engine was running, which we thought was strange, so we knocked on the door." Lo and behold, inside was "one of the most sophisticated electronic systems for cheating I have ever seen—computers, TV cameras, monitors."

It was all part of a blackjack cheating scam, the scope of which stunned gaming control agents. Inside the hotel another gang member was apprehended . . . with a miniature camera hooked to his belt buckle, small computers in both boots, and a tiny headset in his ear through which he received instructions from "master control."

In the old days anyone caught cheating in Las Vegas didn't get the trespass law read to him, and a ride downtown where he posted bail and went on his merry way. He got "thumped." That's the way Roger Mennie put it. "But you can't do that any more. One casino reportedly grabbed some twenty-one cheaters and thumped them, and now they're getting sued for two million dollars." (The case was later settled out of court.)

Cheaters aren't the only ones who get "eighty-sixed" from Las Vegas casinos. Prostitutes aren't welcome, due to the new "family" image, and known felons get the heave-ho whenever they are spotted by surveillance. Eleven of these are members of a rather elite club called The Black Book, put out by the Nevada Gaming Commission. If one of these mobsters gets inside, a Las Vegas hotel can lose its gaming license. There's also another black book that few people outside the casinos know about. It is the work of a former Nevada law enforcement officer, and contains up-to-date mug shots and known scams of some 2,500 undesirables . . . or, at least, whom *he* deems as undesirables. His book service is sold to participating casinos for a rather hefty monthly fee. He has to charge a lot, because he's always getting sued by people who say, "What's *my* picture doing in there?"

He also has a staff of outside security men who roam his client's casino acting like tourists, but what they are really doing is keeping an eye on the people who work there. A word from one of these guys and an employee's job is history.

The hotels also have their own "internal security," and it's similar to the chain of command in the army. The dealers watch the players. The floormen watch the dealers. The pit bosses watch the floormen. The shift boss watches the pit bosses. The eye in the sky watches everybody. Some hotels even employ outside men, whose job is to canvass the whole casino. And now here come the *outside* outside men, working for this one-time policeman. Rest assured the day will come when someone will be watching *them*, too. An outside outside outside man?

They more or less have them already, in the form of agents from the Gaming Control Board.

One of the Board's responsibilities is to count the number of slot machines and gaming tables inside each casino. They're not about to take the casino's word for it since there is a licensing fee for each device. So, if you've ever wondered why some casinos have larger dice tables than others, that's the reason. Casinos do this to cut their fee.

Here is another reason why Control Board members make unannounced visits, as Dunes floorman Eddie Church explains. "They'll take the dice off a table without warning. The dice are put in a sealed envelope and taken to their lab where they are tested for accuracy to determine that they haven't been altered in any way."

Board inspectors may also ask to see some gaming employees' Sheriff's cards, which are required to be in their possession at all times while they are working. Each card has an identification number and a color photo of the employee, and has to be renewed just like a driver's license. In order to get one of these cards, which in reality is a permit to work, the employee must be fingerprinted and pass a thorough police investigation.

Besides making spot checks of their own, agents also investigate complaints filed by unhappy customers. But there always seems to be a rotten apple in the barrel, and this apparently also holds true with state gaming investigators.

One was arrested a year ago while allegedly slipping slugs in a casino slot machine. Another agent reportedly got four stars at Caesars Palace early in 1986—robbery, kidnapping, use of a deadly weapon and assault with a firearm. While working surveillance at Caesars, the agent allegedly followed a high roller and four of his friends to their suite, robbed them, and locked them in a bathroom. Fortunately there was a telephone in the john, and security guards got a phone call before the gaming agent could get out of the hotel.

It all goes back to that human frailty called greed. A lot of people in the casino business don't really like their jobs, unless they have just enough authority to salve their ego. The rest of them are there because of the money. They're certainly not in it for job security—not when a dealer can get fired for "hustling with his eyes." They're most assuredly not in it for the thrill of being around well-heeled gamblers, not when they're drinking and losing their money and getting belligerent. There's no such thing as a feeling of accomplishment, of a job well done.

When the casino is losing money the bosses holler at them, and when the casino is *making* money the players holler at them. The tips dwindle year by year, while the price of everything in the country slowly inches out of reach. The employees see the steady flow of hundred-dollar bills, so crisp they almost crackle—and the expensive clothes and chunky gold watches—and that rosy, well-scrubbed look that only people with money seem to have—and every once in a while one of these employees, who is two months behind on his car payment, gets a tiny germ of an idea. Just once, just a couple of black chips, just enough to get out of the hole so he can sleep at night.

The people who run those gambling casinos aren't dummies. They know all about human nature, that "something for nothing" philosophy that gets people to the tables in the first place. They know there is a touch of larceny in every person. That's why they have the eye in the sky, and outside men or "spotters," and Black Books. How did Bob Brooker put it? ". . . your employee today who is a good solid employee may start running around . . . or having some financial problems . . . and your good employee is no longer good."

It's like the dealer who clapped his hands as he left his post. A friend from out of town asked him, "Why did you clap your hands like that?" The dealer explained, "That's to show I wasn't stealing anything." "Well, who was that fellow standing behind you?" "He's called a floorman. He's there to make sure I don't steal anything." "What's the big black ball hanging over your table?" "That's the camera. It's to make sure I don't steal anything." "Gee," said the dealer's friend, "they don't trust you guys, do they?"

It must be emphasized that 99 percent of all people in the gambling business are honest and upstanding individuals.

"Is stealing by employees really that big a problem?" We asked that question over and over, and the answer—though worded differently—always seems to come out the same. "It'll never be a thing of the past," said one security man. "Because you've got to put in the emotional conflicts that people have in everyday life, and that's what brings people to steal from their employers. It happens to Sears and Roebuck, and it'll always happen in this business."

Jeff Silver, former boss at three top Las Vegas casinos and now a successful attorney, put it bluntly. "When I leave my law office at night and lock the door, I know everything is still going to be there in the morning. I don't have to worry about people stealing from me any more."

How do they do it?

At Caesars Palace, a roulette dealer and a floorman were apprehended for stealing $500 chips. The dealer would slide one of these chips between two stacks of marker buttons near the roulette wheel. The floorman, while pretending to watch the game, would idly shuffle the marker buttons in his hand and then walk away, along with the buttons *and* the $500 chip. No one knows how long this went on.

At another hotel a security guard spotted something unusual while patrolling the property—a small mound of $100 chips underneath a mulberry bush. He stepped into the shadows and waited. Sure enough, a few minutes later a casino boxman showed up to retrieve his "unjust" rewards. He had been taking the chips off the game by sandwiching them underneath the face of his wristwatch.

Dealers have been caught with chips in their pockets, in their mouths, under their belts, in their shoes, up their sleeves, inside their shirts and even in their underwear. In Las Vegas these chips are the same as money. Even as late as the mid-seventies casino tokens could be used at Nevada service stations, laundries and grocery stores. But then one of the largest counterfeiting schemes in Las Vegas history was uncovered, and that was the end of that. Today most casinos won't even interchange chips with other hotels.

This multi-million dollar fraud was pulled off rather easily. The counterfeiters bought thousands of $1 chips from a Reno casino that were identical in color and markings to the $25 chip at a major Las Vegas resort. New $25 inserts were made up and pasted over the old $1 inserts, and the rest was history. The scam might still be going except for the fact that one of the inserts wasn't glued properly and it peeled back along the edges . . . revealing the stomach-lurching "one-dollar" insignia underneath.

Ever wonder why casino dealers wear those funny little aprons while they're working? Management says it's to keep the dealers' slacks from wearing out, but do you think that the people in management *care* whether a dealer's pants wear out or not? Who do they think they're kidding? The real reason for those goofy aprons goes back to "internal security"—to make it a little more difficult for the dealers to "put the five ball in the side pocket."

One shift boss at a Las Vegas casino, who had worked there 20 years, lost his job when he told an over-suspicious new owner, "My dad used to tell me that the person who is always worried about somebody stealing from him is usually a thief himself."

Ironically, the owner who fired him wound up leaving town with the Nevada Gaming Commission hot on his tail—and he has been barred from ever buying another Las Vegas casino.

Said one floorman at Caesars Palace, "You don't have as many dealers stealing any more. Good living stopped it. People have got mortgages on their houses. They're married. Their kids are going to school. And they know if they get caught cheating they're going to be out of a job."

Meanwhile, the cameras keep rolling in the Las Vegas casinos, and the surveillance men keep walking the aisles . . . looking for dealers who violate procedures, and slot cheats, and purse snatchers, and "past-posters." That's someone who sneaks in a bet *after* a winner is established.

New techniques to deter crime are always being introduced. The latest is something called "The Crime Alert Telecomputing System," which will link participating resorts with the police station in Las Vegas through microcomputer terminals. Whenever a suspicious person is spotted, the police will be alerted by the mere pushing of a button.

The most revolutionary innovation in casino surveillance has been the installation of all those cameras, with their refillable loads of video tape. When two major jackpots were hit within a few days of each other at the Frontier and Golden Nugget casinos, gaming agents were able to quickly check the video tapes and verify that the jackpots were legitimate. The tape from the Nugget even showed grandmotherly Ann Bailey of Texas falling off her stool when she struck the $1.8 million jackpot.

The need for the cameras on the major slot machines was clearly displayed, however, by two federal court trials involving organized slot cheating rings. One, headed by a Las Vegan, took the casinos for 3.25 million. The other, led by two brothers from California, is said to have "won" six luxury cars and almost a quarter of a million dollars in cash between 1976 and 1979.

Four people are now awaiting trial for enlisting the aid of a dealer to make a false cut on a deck of cards, which was captured on camera. The eye in the sky also caught a group of organized cheaters who had been changing their bets after the ball quit bouncing on the roulette table. This happened at the Marina, according to security chief Tom Shellabarger, and resulted in the table being redesigned.

Sometimes the tapes can be used to keep the customer happy over a dispute. Say a gambler is drinking heavily during a spirited craps game. He may forget he signed a marker at one point, and playing back the tape can resolve the problem and make him happy again. Or as happy as he can be under the circumstances. He's still going to feel rotten once he sobers up.

"I did *what?*"

The men who watch those little black-and-white TV monitors eight hours a day don't have a very glamorous job. It can get pretty boring looking out for nervous nellies, or known cheats that are usually on their toes anyway. A former "monitor" in one of the casinos said he whiled away his hours by looking for babes in low-cut dresses. He said the zoom controls on the cameras "were everything they were cracked up to be." Maybe that's why he is a *former* TV monitor now.

One of those still in the surveillance game is Les Weidenfeld, the "I Spy" of the Tropicana. When asked how he spent his offhours at home after being glued to those TV monitors, Weidenfeld said, "I like to watch television." With a laugh he added, "I tell people it's because I miss the commercials during the daytime."

CHAPTER 4

The Games

"Nevada and New Jersey attract the dregs of humanity, the scum of life, the used coffee grounds of society. They are home to every known kind of gangster, deviant, Mafia hit person, pervert, neurotic, psychotic, godfather businessman, drug addict and second-rate nightclub entertainer." *(Florida Times-Union)*

Used coffee grounds? Mafia hit person? Apparently some dime-head columnist at the Florida Times-Union wears a size 2 hat. That was Las Vegas TV reporter Ned Day's response to the Florida attack. But there *are* people who don't like the things Las Vegas stands for, people who think the only time the lights dim in this neon fairyland is in commemoration of Bugsy Siegel's birthday.

Well, 14.2 million people don't think so. That's the number of tourists and conventioneers who visited Vegas in 1985, a new record for the Nevada city. They threw around a lot of money, $7.2 billion in all, most of it in the casinos. They didn't actually think they were throwing their money away; they were under the impression that they were gambling. Paying their money and taking their chances at blackjack, keno, roulette, craps, baccarat, the Big Six, slot machines, sports books, and a couple of Oriental whodunits called Sic Bo and Pai Gow.

In this chapter we will explore these games of risk, and maybe then you will have a better idea who pays for those chintzy chandeliers and cushiony carpeting. By the way, ever wonder what happens to the old carpet when the casinos roll out new rugs? It isn't scrapped, but sold to restaurants and the like. The hotels rarely give anything away for free; try to get a comp to the show some night. At one time used dice and cards were passed out freely to anyone who asked for them. Now they're sold to gift shops and souvenir stands. A penny saved is a penny earned. Corporation logic.

All right. On now to the games people play!

Roulette

This gambling gambit had its origins in France a couple of centuries back. Though just about everyone knows how to play . . . "just follow the bouncing ball" . . . it's really not all that popular in this country. In fact, less than two percent of the people who come to Las Vegas even stop at the wheel. That's why there is seldom more than one roulette table in a casino. The people who run casinos would rather fill up the place with hordes of hungry slot machines.

Each player uses different colored chips, so there's no confusion as to whose bets are whose. The chips are worth a quarter a piece or however much the player wishes up to the casino's limit. The wheel has 38 slots, numbered 1 through 36, plus a green-colored 0 and 00. Bets are made until the ball just about drops from its track, and the dealer calls "no more bets."

How do you bet and what do you get? Half the 36 numbers are red and half are black, so if you bet the winning color you get even money. It's also an even money payoff when you:

A. Bet the winning number is odd or even

B. Bet the winning number is from 1 to 18 or 19 to 36

Then the odds start to climb a little bit. Bet in groups of 12 numbers for a 2-1 payoff, or straight up on any one number—including 0 and 00—to get 35-1. Bet two numbers with one chip, which is called a split, and the payoff drops down to 17-1. Another popular bet is the "corner," which covers four numbers in a group, and that payoff is 8-1.

It sounds complicated, but it's not. No gambling game is really that complex, otherwise no one would play it. Some games are just a little intimidating, and that's what scares the bejesus out of would-be craps shooters. It is the main reason slot machines are so popular. (1) Put coin in slot, (2) Pull handle, (3) Wire home for more money.

But getting back to roulette, the main drawback to this game is that ominous 0, and 00. These two "partners in crime " give the house a decided advantage, more so than in Europe where there is only one 0 on the wheel.

Using a one-number bet as an example, the true odds are 37 to 1, since there are 38 numbers on the wheel. But you are only paid 35 to 1. So even when you win you lose. If your bet was a dollar, you wound up losing two dollars when you won! It is what is known as the house edge, and it comes to 5.26 percent. In plain English, that means the casino expects to keep $5.26 of every $100 that goes on the table.

Worst bet on the roulette table? All of them.

Best bet? Well, there *is* one way of winning, according to gambling author John Gollehon. Gollehon, who has written almost a dozen books on gambling, believes that roulette dealers develop a rhythmic style . . . much like a golfer's swing . . . after spinning that little ball for so many years. "He will let go of the ball at precisely the same spots on the wheel-head, and over a period of time will actually wear a groove in the track. To counter this, most casinos will rotate the wheel-head a few inches every week or so, to prevent a groove from forming."

A Las Vegas roulette boss backed up Gollehon's theory, citing a recent instance at a London casino where a gang took the roulette game for millions of dollars. After watching the dealer's move for a few hours the information on his "deliverance" was fed into a computer, and the house edge flew out the house window. Vegas casinos have already been alerted to be on the lookout for the same bunch.

TRIVIA: A roulette wheel weighs 100 pounds. A high-quality wheel costs $4800, and the table itself another $1800.

Keno

Keno's first name was "Chinese Lottery." Indeed, that's what it was when developed in China about 1000 B.C. Legend has it that keno financed the building of the Great Wall.

Keno tickets are in two sections, numbers 1 through 40 in the top section, and 41 through 80 in the bottom section. This reflects the Oriental "Yin and Yang" division. The game was introduced to the United States by Chinese immigrants in coastal ports around the turn of the century, with 120 Chinese characters to choose from that were painted on maple balls.

But keno *was* a lottery, and Nevada law—even after

gambling was enacted— forbid lotteries. So the name "Chinese Lottery" got changed to "Race-Horse Keno," as a clever deception by using the names of then famous race horses along with the actual numbers. Then the U.S. government passed a law taxing off-track betting, and the casinos—afraid they might get *their* "yin" in a "yang"— changed the name again. Since 1951 the game has just been called Keno.

In the United States, it's only legal in the state of Nevada; you won't find it in Atlantic City or anywhere else. Like all other casino games it has been completely Americanized. It's strictly a numbers game now, using 80 high-class ping-pong balls and a thingamajig call a "goose" that sucks up 20 of the balls at random. It is an easy game to play, it is cheap, and you've got an outside chance of winning $50,000. One big drawback to keno is trying to keep from nodding off to sleep while the game gets underway. One tourist said that playing keno was "like watching somebody iron a T-shirt."

The object of the game is to try to guess which 20 of those 80 numbers is going to pop up on the keno board. You don't have to guess all 20, either. Pick one for $3, and if it shows up you win $9. Pick two and one won't win anything, but *both* will get you $36. Get eight out of eight and pocket a cool fifty thousand. These are called straight tickets. There are also split tickets, way tickets, combination tickets and special tickets. Information on all of them is available at your friendly neighborhood keno parlor.

The game is so simple, and the payoffs are oftentimes so stupefying, that it seems there is no way to lose. One-fourth of the 80 numbers come up in every single game; get eight of the 20 of the 80 and win a fortune. Nothing to it. Nothing to it?

Better sit down for this one. The odds of picking eight out of eight are 230,114 to one! Since the minimum bet to win the big jackpot is usually three dollars, you should be winning the grand sum of $693,342. So what's the casino going to pay you if you ever did manage to pull off an 8-out-of-8? A *paltry* $50,000. The check they give you probably says, "Pay to the order of Stupid." You're only getting shorted by six hundred thousand and some pocket change.

The more numbers you try to catch the greater the odds. Nailing ten out of ten is nearly a 9 million-to-one long shot; 12 out of 12 is almost 500,000,000 to 1! And if all that isn't enough, the casinos have what they call an "aggregate" payoff, not to be confused with "aggravate." That means if the heavens should part, and *two* people hit a $50,000 ticket in the same game, they would have to split the pot and settle for $25,000 each. It's like a slap in the face with a wet sock.

One other thing to remember in playing keno: the casinos keep your initial bet. If you hit a one-spot ticket for $3, you should get back $12—since the true odds are 3 to 1 against you. But you only get back $9, three dollars of which was yours to begin with. This changes the odds to 2 to 1, and sends the player to the poorhouse a percentage point at a time.

So why do people bang their beans against this bingo-like bamboozler? John Gollehon says it's because "keno is a cheap game. A player can spend as little as seventy cents on a ticket and wait 15 minutes to see whether he won or not. What other game gives you that kind of 'action' for your money?"

The house advantage in keno breaks down to at least 25 percent over the course of all payout possibilities, and—

next to the slot machines—should be the casino's biggest money maker. But the men behind the tables dislike the game for the same reasons players love it . . . the length of time it takes to play, the chickenfeed bets, the cost of supplies, and the payroll for all those keno runners and keno writers and ball-tumblers and supervisors. Bob Brooker of the Marina says it's really a tough game to make money on.

Worst bet? The long shots.

Best bet? A four-spot or six-spot ticket, pooling some of your favorite numbers, or birthdays, or anniversary dates. You may not win anything, but at least the game becomes a little more personal.

TRIVIA: Each keno ticket clearly states that "Winning tickets must be collected immediately after each keno game is called." Miss the deadline, and your winnings go to an old people's home in Schenectady.

Craps

It's the fastest game in town, and the most exciting. Introduced from Europe to New Orleans in the 1800's, this dice game reached its peak of popularity in World War II. That's when American GIs discovered it, and it's still a casino favorite.

The layout looks complicated until you realize that both ends of the table have the same diagrams, and the middle is filled with proposition bets, which you're better off not knowing about anyway. There are four people who run the game. The boxman, sitting in the middle behind the table, watches the dice . . . settles all disputes . . . and crams all the money in the box, hence his name "boxman." The two dealers, one on each side of him, pay off the bets on their section of the table. The stickman, who stands on the player's side of the table, controls the pace of the game and barks out the numbers as they roll. He is called a stickman because of the limber bamboo pole he uses to push the dice to the shooter. Other equipment of the game includes the dice bowl, where spare dice are kept; the puck, which marks the point during each hand; and the marker buttons, sometimes know as "lammers," which are used to keep track of call bets and IOU's.

To start a hand, the shooter selects two dice and rolls them across the table so that they hit the wall at the other end. If he rolls 7 or 11 he wins whatever he bet on the "Pass Line." If he throws a 2, 3 or 12 he has rolled a "craps" and he loses his "Pass Line" bet. He hasn't lost the dice, though—just his money and his friends.

If he rolls a 4, 5, 6, 8, 9 or 10 that becomes the "point" and he must roll that number again *before* he rolls a 7. And that's it.

The most important thing to remember about craps is that at no time are you betting with or against the *house*; you are betting with or against the *dice*. If you bet with the dice or with the shooter, bet on the "Pass Line." To bet against the dice, bet on the "Don't Pass."

When betting the "Pass Line" you should take the odds, once a point is established. This money, up to double the amount you have on the "Pass Line" (in casinos that have double odds) goes behind your original bet, and pays you the true house odds on any point number. It's the only fair bet in the casino! You get two to one if the point is 4 or 10; three to two if the point is 5 or 9; and six to five if the point is 6 or 8.

"Come Bets" are also popular if the shooter is rolling

lots of numbers. This money "comes" to the next number thrown, with the same rules that apply to "Pass Line" bets. And you can take the odds on these bets, too.

But in craps, as in any other Las Vegas game, the house has the edge. From .63 percent for a "Pass Line" or "Come" bet to 1.41 depending on the amount if any, of your odds bet. Then it starts to climb. From 4 percent for a "Place Bet" on the five or nine to 16.67 percent on an "Any Seven" one-roll bet.

Here's another one of those examples of how you lose even when you win. The odds of a twelve rolling are 35 to one. If one rolls, and you have $1 bet on it, you get paid 30 *for* 1 at Las Vegas Strip casinos. Your dollar is left on 12 for another roll without your permission. So instead of walking away from the table with $35 profit, you limp off with $29, six dollars gouged out of your hide by the casino and you were a *winner!*

Another advantage the house has is that no hand in a craps game should really last very long. According to the law of averages, a 7 should show once in every six rolls. It doesn't always work that way, but that's what the casino *expects.*

Something bad is happening, though, to the game of craps in Las Vegas. Dice tables along the Strip won a record $242,950,000 during 1979-80, but it's been declining each year since then. The win percentage* is still a respectable

---

*The "win percentage, or "drop" percentage as the casinos routinely call it, should not be confused with the house percentage of each game. The win percentages represent that portion of the player's money that the casino will win *because* of the house percentage. It's more correctly a measure of the amount of a player's original stake that the player will ultimately part with, by playing on and on. Casinos like to think that nearly all games generate a 20% drop percentage for the house.

The casino's "advantage" in the games is correctly called the *house* percen-

18 percent, but in fiscal 1984-85 the tables only netted $194,767,000. This has caused some casino veterans to say that craps is a dying game on the Strip. Why? Because a good many of the most avid players were from the East and are now spending more time at Atlantic City casinos.

The win percentage* in downtown Las Vegas was only 14.1 percent for the 84-85 fiscal year. That has been attributed to more "savvy" on the part of the players, and the heavy use of multiple odds—as high as 10 times your bet at the Horseshoe.

Worst bet on the dice table? Proposition bets.

Best bet? A wager on the "Pass Line," with as much odds as you can get. And two "Come Bets," with the odds.

Author John Gollehon says there is another way of winning at craps. It's based on what he calls the "gyroscope principle." He says, "A good dice 'mechanic' can control the dice so that they spin in a certain rotation after leaving his hand." This helps to "eliminate dice combinations that give the house an advantage." Does it work? Gollehon says the man who perfected this "curve ball" has been barred from Vegas casinos. (Gollehon has a book underway about this phenomena, titled "Winner Take All," due in bookstores in the spring of 1987.)

TRIVIA: It takes fourteen different operations to manufacture casino dice, which are made of cellulose acetate. They are accurate within 1/10,000th of an inch, or

tage, such as 5.26% for roulette. The house percentage applies to each and every decision on the tables; each roll, each spin, each toss, each hand. The drop percentage is always much higher than the house percentage because most players play too long, letting the small house percentage eat away at their stake, and eventually take a large portion of it (generally 20%), or all of it, if the player has no concept of quitting. In that case, the drop percentage would be 100%. That's why casinos love players who chain themselves to the tables.

like splitting a hair on your head twenty times! Dice cost $2.50 a pair, and they are changed three times a day on each table. Opposite sides of the dice always add up to seven. The one-spot on the dice has the casino name or insignia on it, and the number of the dice is stamped on the two-spot. This is so the dice can always be checked quickly by the boxman or floorman. Incidentally, the casino refers to a single dice as "dice." The term "die," although correct, isn't used.

Pai Gow And Sic Bo

牌九是美國骨牌的前身，玩法是以一套三十二只的骨牌排列成最佳的組合配答。般賣的玩法是玩者預測勝利的組合，若盈用之三粒骰子所擲示的總和或個別點數與預測的組合相同為勝。

Translation:
PAI GOW is the predecessor of American dominoes. The object of the game is to set the 32 dominoes into pairs for the best ranking combinations. SIC BO is played with three dice, and the object is to select winning combinations, which are brightly illuminated on the layout.

The Big Six

Everyone has been to a carnival. Some have had the fillings in their teeth pulled out by candied apples, and others have had the fillings in their wallets pulled out by *bad* apples who run the rube-fleecing wheels of fortune.

Those clickety clickety come-ons are still around. Only now they're found in Las Vegas casinos, and they go by flashy names like "The Money Wheel" and "The Big Six." It's called The Big Six because there are six different payoffs you can get, depending on which of the 54 slots on the wheel comes around. There are 23 $1 slots; 15 $2 slots; eight $5 slots; four $10 slots; two $20 slots; one joker and one casino slot. If the wheel stops on a "five," for example, and you have a bet on it, you'll be paid off at the rate of $5 to every $1 that you bet. And so on. The two big ones, the joker and the casino slot, each pay off at 40 to 1, but they must be bet separately.

The players bet, the dealer spins the wheel, the players leave, the dealer puts their money in the box. It's so simple even a child could play it. Come to think of it, who else would want to? The house advantage is 14.8 percent even on the one dollar slots, and spirals upward to 24 percent on the joker and casino slots. Say you bet $10 on the joker, and the joker turns up. (Jokers are always turning up in the casinos anyhow.) The joker is a 53 to 1 dark horse, so you should get back $530. What do you get? Four hundred dollars.

Guess who pockets the other hundred and thirty.

Worst bet on The Big Six? The joker slot, and the casino slot.

Best bet? The Wayne Newton show.

TRIVIA: A Big Six wheel, complete with two layouts, costs $6800. This includes real currency that is displayed on both the wheel and under the glass on the layouts. The bills shown amount to $249.

Slot Machines

Want to win a million dollars? Stick three bucks in a slot machine. That's what a woman did at Caesars Palace. She had gone to a show and she was tired, but her friends persuaded her to stay up. Browsing through the casino she stopped at a progressive slot, dropped three one-dollar tokens into it, and lined up a row of sevens to win $1,065,358.

A Texas electrician won $92,000 the very first time he ever pulled the handle of a slot machine in Las Vegas. He was "shocked." But a housewife who hit $11,000 on another machine said she had been playing it for two *months* before she finally won.

Or look what happened to Maurice Fuoco of New Hampshire. He lined up a row of identical symbols at the Mint Hotel, and the overhead electronic display said his jackpot was $172,000. Sorry, said the Mint, computer error. The jackpot tally should have read $327.95. Cases like this, involving machine malfunctions, are now being decided in the courts.

But exactly what *is* a slot machine, and what are your chances of beating this one-armed bandit? The nickname alone is enough to give you some idea of where you stand. Up until the 1960s Nevada slot machines were purely mechanical, coins were played one at a time, there was a single pay-line, and if you were lucky you might win a hundred dollars or so. The machines had three reels and you tried to line up things like cherries and oranges and watermelons. Get a lemon and you were an automatic loser, and that's where the term "lemon" originated for any bad piece of merchandise.

Then came the Space Age, and the old hand-cranked slot machines became museum pieces. Today's machines feature such modern technology as CRT video screens, integrated circuits, silicon chips to deter tampering, microprocessors to control the reels, and random access generators that can be programmed in any of 4,000 different modes, or percentages. About the only thing old and new slot machines have in common is that they both accept *money.*

If variety is the spice of life, today's slot players are well-seasoned indeed. They can choose from single pay-lines, multiple pay-lines, progressive slots, and video slots such as poker, keno and blackjack. Most gaming bosses behind the tables see these video slot machines, which swallow up to five quarters at a time, as the game of the future in Las Vegas. Really, the percentages aren't that bad, and you can play at your own pace without somebody glaring at you or giving you exasperated looks. Play keno for 75 cents and kill fifteen minutes! How about spending your whole two-week vacation sitting at a video blackjack machine for a dollar and a quarter? "Should I take a card; should I stand?" And don't forget the free drinks.

Somebody is putting an awful lot of money in Las Vegas slot machines. An *awful* lot. Said our man at Summa, which owns six Vegas resorts, "At least 50 percent of any casino's profit is generated by the slot machines. If you'll look at the statistics you'll see that slots have taken the most progressive leap forward. And your labor costs are not that significant."

In the first three months of 1985 gaming revenue in Las Vegas and county was nearly $574 million, up $53.5 million over the first quarter of the preceding year. That means that a little over $286 million went into the slot machines, and stayed there. And that's just for the first three months of the year!

What's really frightening is how the Vegas casinos boast about their slot payoffs on the marquees. "OUR SLOTS GUARANTEE 94% RETURN." What they are saying is that for every dollar you stick in one of their slot machines, you're going to get 94 cents back. Put a hundred dollars in, get ninety-four dollars. And the casinos are *advertising* it.

In other words, these machines that give a 94% return have a "hold" of six percent. Put simply, the casino will hold, or keep, six percent of all coins fed into it. In Las Vegas most nickel slots hold from 15 to 20 percent; quarter machines hold eight to twelve percent; and dollar machines hold anywhere from three to ten percent. To keep the dollar players happy you have to give them some of their money back in frequent payoffs. Otherwise these high rollers of the slot machine game will take their paper cups across the street.

You have to give them jackpots, too. Big jackpots! Stupendous jackpots! That's the lure of the gaudy, bell-ringing, siren-wailing progressive slot machines . . . the ones with the hundred thousand dollar and million dollar jackpots.

Of course, the bigger the bonanza, the greater the odds of hitting it. Most of the big money machines have five reels, and each reel has 25 stops on it, with only one winning symbol on each reel. That makes the odds of becoming an instant millionaire 9,765,624 to one! In order to get the big prize you have to insert the maximum number of dollars, which would be $3.00 worth. It's almost too mind-blowing to put down on ordinary paper, but if you hit a million dollar jackpot with an investment of $3.00 you should get back—based on the percentages—the grand sum of $29,296,872! So what do you get? Not twenty-nine million, that's for sure. In fact, the biggest jackpot ever hit was at Harrah's at Lake Tahoe, and that was only 2.5 million dollars.

Even when some lucky devil wins a million the casino isn't paying him off. Not really. The money is actually paid by all the other players who lost. According to John Gollehon's excellent book "All About Slots And Video Poker"—"A common practice in many casinos with the big-money carousels is to remove 10% of the handle (all money wagered) each day and place this money in an escrow account. The casino is not saving this money for themselves . . . the casino is in fact saving the money for the ultimate winner."

Even bigger jackpots are on the horizon. There's one called Megabucks which is now being tested at three Nevada casinos. It calls for more than 100 slot machines at a number of casinos throughout the state to be linked by a Reno computer, with an eventual jackpot of up to $15 million. Planners see it as "logical competition" to the huge lottery jackpots operated by a number of states including California.

Worst bet on the slots? Nickel machines.

Best bet? Video poker, because of player options. Just remember, though that the odds of making a royal flush—which pays the big prize—are about 40,000 to 1.

TRIVIA: A slot machine weighs 200 pounds. New electronic machines from Bally go for $4900. Slots are emptied of coins once a day in large casinos, twice a week at the smaller places.

Poker

Poker is legal in Gardena, California, and it's legal in the state of Nevada. It's strictly a game of skill, so if you don't want to find yourself going heads-up against somebody like Johnny Moss or Amarillo Slim you'd better stick to Saturday night sessions with your friends.

The big games in Las Vegas poker rooms are 7 card stud, 7 card low, Hi-low split, Hi-low split with eights or better, Hold 'em, and Omaha, which is a deviation of Hold 'em. There's also Hold 'em limit, Hold 'em pot limit and Hold 'em no limit. Hold 'em is played by dealing two cards facedown to the players, three face-up in the middle of the table for all players to use, and then two more face-down to each player. Bets are made on the "flop" of each card.

The house makes its money by taking 10 percent of the pot, three dollar maximum. This is called the "rake." In big games this rule is waived, and the table is charged a flat $75 an hour.

But if you "know when to bluff 'em and know when to stuff 'em" you can overcome the house edge and go home a winner.

Worst bet? A small game, because of the rake.

Best bet? Playing video poker.

TRIVIA: Poker rooms use plastic playing cards, while paper cards are used for other casino games. Plastic cards are much more expensive . . . $7 a deck as compared with

90¢ to $1.20 for paper cards with logo. But plastic cards last longer; they're kept clean by washing with soda water.

Baccarat

Think of baccarat and what image comes to mind? Big hills of hundred dollar bills? Tall suntanned dealers in snappy black tuxes? A private little casino with an elegant softly-lit sign that whispers BACCARAT? A *big* security guard standing next to the velvet rope? "Move along, buddy." "But officer, I was just—" "Move *along*, buddy." "Uhh, yes sir."

Hey, wait a minute. This is America, and this is the twentieth century. If you want to play baccarat, then do it! It's the most underrated game in town. It offers the best odds of winning, it's played at a nice easy pace, and there's no one screaming in your ear or spilling something on your shoes. It's like a vacation in the country; it's like Central Park in the middle of New York City; it's the game you've got to play at least once in your life just so you can say you did it.

First, a brief history lesson. In the 1500s the French aristocrats didn't have anything to do, so they made up a game which they called Baccara. It's still popular in many countries, along with two variations of the game: Chemin De Fer and Baccarat, or "Punto Banco," as it's known abroad.

The first thing you have to learn about baccarat is how to pronounce it. If you say "Back-a-rat" you will have exposed yourself as a *tourist*. But if you say "Bah-cah-rah" that big security guard by the velvet rope is going to move right out of your way.

The baccarat table seats twelve players and two dealers,

one on each side. Their job is to take losers and pay winners. A third dealer stands on the other side of the table. He calls the cards and passes the "shoe" after each hand. The shoe is a wooden or plastic box holding eight decks of cards, and is exactly like the shoes used in most Las Vegas blackjack games.

The object of baccarat is to achieve a total of nine with two cards or an additional third card if necessary. All number cards 2 through 9 count as their face value; aces count as 1; and all 10-value cards, including face cards, count as 0. For instance, a jack and a four would count as 0 plus 4, or 4.

The shoe passes around the table in a counter-clockwise direction after each hand. Participants may bet with either the "player" or with the "banker," who is the fellow that gets to slide the cards out of the shoe. Even the "banker" can bet with the "player" if he wants to; being the "banker" is just part of the ceremony.

Now we're ready to begin. "Card for the player," the dealer intones. Out slides a card, face-down, which the dealer keeps in the middle of the table. "Card for the banker." This card is tucked under the shoe by the banker. "Card for the player." Sounds like a scene from a James Bond movie. "Card for the banker."

The dealer then gives the two unexposed cards in the middle of the table to the player having the largest bet on the player's side, who turns them over and tosses them back to the dealer. The banker exposes his cards, and the following rules prevail:

If the player's cards total 8 or 9, the players automatically win; that's called a "natural." *Unless* the banker's total ties the player's total; in that case the hand is played over. The player must stand if a 6 or 7 total comes up; and the banker, if he has less than 6, might draw an additional card, subject to "third card rules."

There is one proposition bet on the table, and that is the "ties." If the player and banker end up with the same amount, and you bet the tie, you will get nine for one.

Just remember, in Nevada baccarat the house banks all bets, so you are not playing against any other player, but against the house. The casino has a 1.06% edge on the banker's hand, and a 1.24% edge on the player's hand, so it's natural to assume you're better off betting with the banker. But the casino charges a commission of 5% of your winnings, should you bet the bank side and win. This can lead to problems for a player betting with the bank when he decides to quit. His "vigorish" for all those banker bets that he won is still on the table, and it's time to settle up. However, he may have lost 50 bets and won only ten, and as he starts to walk away in a daze—wondering if perhaps there is a diving board on the roof of the hotel—the dealer says, "Excuse me, sir, but there is the matter of your $3,000 commission."

Worst bet at baccarat? Betting on ties. The odds are 14.1 against you.

Best bet? Siding with the banker. Even with the commission, the house edge is only 1.06%

TRIVIA: Baccara is Italian for "zero." The minimum bet at baccarat is usually $20, and the max is $2,000 unless your last name is Rockefeller. Playing cards are ordered in lots of 100,000 decks. Layouts cost $60 and are changed every two to three months depending on use.

Blackjack

Las Vegas visitors spend a third of their gambling time

at the blackjack tables. It's also called Twenty-One, and sometimes losers refer to it as Twenty-Two. It got the name Blackjack because in its early years players were rewarded extra if they got an ace of spades and a jack of spades as their first two cards.

Because it is a card game of counting points and having showdowns, blackjack is a little bit like baccarat, only instead of trying to get nine points the player tries to get closer to 21 than the dealer. If the player gets higher than 21 he has "busted" and loses.

An ace counts 1 or 11, as the player chooses. The numbered cards 2 through 10 count at face value, and picture cards count as ten. A "Blackjack" is an ace and any ten-value card, and pays 3 to 2, unless the dealer also gets one. Then it's a "push" and neither wins.

The dealer must stand on any hand that totals between 17 and 21, and must "hit" any hand under 17. But the big drawback to blackjack for the player is that he must hit his hand *first*, if he's not satisfied with his first two cards. This gives the casino a hefty 7 percent advantage.

But the player has a few things going for him, too:

SPLITTING: He can split identical pairs in his hand and double his bet in the process.

DOUBLING DOWN: He can double his bet after seeing his original two cards, and get *one* extra card from the dealer.

INSURANCE: He can bet half of his original wager to "insure" his original bet, when the dealer has an ace showing. If, in fact, the dealer does have a ten card "in the hole," the player who has taken insurance will lose his original bet, but win 2 to 1 on the other wager. Still, insurance is *not* a smart bet.

SURRENDER: If he doesn't like his first two cards the

player can surrender his hand for one-half of his bet. Some people like this option, and some people don't. One argument is that if a player is going to give up half his bet, then why doesn't he just bet half as much to start with? And one player was heard telling his wife, "Why don't we surrender *every* hand, and that way we'll be able to play twice as long!" Again, quoting John Gollehon, "Surrender is indeed an advantage to the player, over long-term play, and all serious players should look for it. Unfortunately, few casinos can be found where surrender is offered. Surprised?"

The average house percentage in most Las Vegas blackjack pits is between four and five percent, taking into account good, bad, and very bad players. Of all the money risked, the house expects to keep between 18 and 19 percent as their "drop" percentage.   (see footnote on page 68.)

This percentage used to be higher, but players are more sophisticated these days with betting strategies they have learned from experts like Ken Uston, Edward Thorp and John Gollehon. Even some of the *casinos* hold free classes on how to play blackjack . . . including the Imperial Palace, Las Vegas Hilton and Stardust. But Gollehon says you get what you pay for, and even though "the potential for new blackjack players is one hundred times the current number" these learning sessions held by the casinos are "almost like leading sheep to slaughter."

One thing that Thorp did in his book "Beat The Dealer," and that Gollehon introduced in his bestseller "Pay The Line," was to instruct blackjack players on how to count cards. The theory, originally worked out by IBM computer expert Julian Braun, kept track of how many small cards were left in the deck (advantageous to the casino) and how many big cards were left (advantageous to the player). The casinos countered the counters by changing to multiple decks of cards, dealt out of shoes. But some counters are so good at what they do that they've got the house at a disadvantage—up to two percent! When the house is on the receiving end for a change, it's grounds for divorce in Las Vegas. Consequently, some card-counters find their 8-by-10s in those casino "black books."

Card counters—according to law professor I. Nelson Rose—"pose the greatest threat to the financial health of a casino." In his book *Gambling And The Law,* Rose writes:

"With perfect card counting and perfect rules, such as a single deck dealt down to the last card and the unlimited right to vary the size of bets, it becomes a statistical certainty that the player, not the house, will win in the long run—if the player has enough money to last through short-term losing streaks."

The most popular method of counting cards is by assigning a "plus" number to the small cards that have been played, and a "minus" number to aces and all ten-value cards. Not counted are 7's, 8's and 9's. So, if you see five little cards and three big ones, you have a plus-2 count, and you bet accordingly.

This system is commonly referred to as a "point count" and it is regarded as the most powerful. Here is a chart that simplifies a typical point-count strategy:

PLUS (COUNT +1)					MINUS (COUNT −1)				
2	3	4	5	6	7	8	9	10	A
1	1	1	1	1	0	0	0	1	1

When counting systems were first introduced, mail order come-ons were a dime a dozen, but gamblers paid anywhere from $200 to $500 for them. The ads spelled it all out. "Easy to learn, simple to use." "Will enable you to play as well as any expert." "You will win under ANY conditions." These systems were money-makers, all right—for the people who wrote them. Usually, all the customer got were three or four pages of computer readouts and a sheaf of mimeographed copies of basic card strategy.

Suddenly every player who sat down at a Vegas black-jack table was a card counter. Behind the tables, paranoia and hysteria set in.

The casinos retaliated. Six-deck shoes were introduced. No card counter could keep track of over three hundred cards. But they could, and they did. Then the casinos realized they had privileged gaming licenses, and that they could bar anyone they wanted from playing in their establishments. If the player had the advantage, the house didn't want his business. It was as simple as that.

Las Vegas emptied every gun in its arsenal. Casino bosses learned how to detect counters. If somebody was betting $15 on every hand dealt, and then suddenly made a $400 wager, the cards were shuffled immediately. If he pulled back his bet while the cards were being shuffled, surveillance was notified and the player would be watched carefully. Sometimes he turned out to be a "hunch bettor," and no further action was taken. But if it was determined that the player in question was indeed a card counter, out the door he went.

A floor supervisor at one Strip casino tells about the player who lost $6,000 at one of the blackjack games she was watching. "I went up to him and gave him my card, and asked him where he was staying. He said, 'I don't have a room.' 'Stay with us,' I told him. Later I found out that not only was he a counter, but that his picture was in one of our black books. And I comped his room!'' She laughed when she told the story, remembering how she learned from a casino security man that the player was a counter. Her reply to him was, "We need more card counters. He was the only guy we beat all day."

Some of the most recent schemes in Las Vegas by counters involve teams of players. A blackjack boss explains how one group of these counters operate:

"These people sit at the game, playing the minimum bet, and they count the shoe down. The 'money man' walks around the casino, and when he gets a signal from his friends he zooms in and starts playing. He hasn't been at the game, so he can't be accused of being a counter. It's very, very dangerous."

A Blackjack dealer remembers the time a noted card counter sat down at the table, where he proceeded to lose practically every bet he made. He would double-down on a fourteen, for example, and laugh uproariously when he lost. The supervisors were so busy watching the counter that they paid no attention to the other players at the table, all of whom won bet after bet. It turned out that all of these players, including the famous card counter, were working *together* . . . with the counter cuing the others by his signals.

Counters maintain that they are doing nothing wrong. They play by the rules as set up by the casino regulators and the casinos themselves. Even in 1983, in a Nevada court case, the court had this to say:

". . . A card counter—one who uses a point system to keep track of the cards that have been played—does not alter any of the basic features of the game. He merely uses his mental skills to take advantage of the same information that is available to the public.''

Be that as it may, the Federal Court ruled that the state of Nevada was not a partner to a private company (casinos) and therefore the constitutional rights of card counters had not been violated.

So the dealers keep shuffling those cards, sometimes after just two or three hands. Counters smile thinly and head for greener pastures, but meanwhile the game has been slowed and that means less profit for the casino. To combat this, several resorts in Las Vegas have instituted something called a "roving shuffler." This is a blackjack dealer who works behind a podium with wheels on it, and all he does is shuffle cards. As soon as the shoe on one table is depleted, he is right there with a fresh one. If a suspected card counter is playing, the "roving shuffler" will be at hand, with as many new shoes of cards as the dealer needs.

Constantly shuffling the cards has been proven to be the best way of thwarting counters, so it will probably be used until the next Ice Age. Most of the time the supervisor will signal the dealer to re-shuffle by either nodding to the dealer or whispering instructions in his ear.

A few years back there was one pit boss who had his own way of signaling the dealer. He would tap the dealer on the seat of his pants. A cocktail waitress once watched him do this, and thought it was so funny that she went through the entire blackjack pit . . . tapping every dealer "behind" the tables. The dealers reacted like mechanized automatons, all stopping their games at the same time to re-shuffle the cards. It was almost five minutes before another hand of blackjack got underway. The next day the cocktail waitress was hustling drinks in the keno lounge.

The year was 1978. Card counters had more or less been expelled from Nevada casinos. Those green pastures they were seeking were in a steamy, sultry seaside town called Atlantic City. It was a card counter's paradise.

Atlantic City blackjack tables had been using multiple decks of cards, and by constant re-shuffling casino bosses figured card counters would be kept at bay. But then in 1979 the New Jersey Casino Control Commission changed the rules—no shuffling of the cards until most of them had been used. Revenue fell. With less than one hundred black-jack tables in the whole state of New Jersey, it did not take that many card counters to send Resorts International reeling. Resorts was the only hotel open at the time, and the counters were bankrupting it . . . or so it claimed.

Someone got an idea. Suppose card counters were barred from the casino? "It worked in Las Vegas, didn't it?" Paul Burst, Executive Vice-President of Del Webb's Claridge Casino, finishes the story:

"We were allowed to bar card counters up to September of 1982. That's when the statute in New Jersey was successfully challenged and the courts ordered the casinos to change their regulations which previously barred card counters."

Six-deck shoes were replaced with eight-deck shoes. Betting limits were lowered in most casinos. Where gamblers could once bet up to $2,000 on a turn of the cards, the top wager now was suddenly $500, or in some cases $100. "But nothing happened," said Burst. "The financial picture didn't change." In fact, it got better. Gross casino revenues in Atlantic City went from $1.9 billion in 1982 to $2.2 billion the following year. And, to no one's great surprise, Resorts International never did go bankrupt.

Card counters are still free to roam through the casinos

in Atlantic City. However, regulations have been loosened so that the house keeps the edge. Back is the "discretionary shuffle rule," as it is called in New Jersey. Shoes are again down to six decks of cards, and the Claridge recently used sixteen billboards advertising its new four-deck shoes.

Other policies employed by Atlantic City casinos include the restriction of the maximum amount that a player can bet "in certain situations." Infrequently, a player will be held to one betting spot on the table, and sometimes a player will not be allowed on a blackjack game until the cards in the shoe have been re-shuffled. According to Burst, this is to discourage players who are "shadow counts," which is a card counter who stands back and waits for the deck to be in his favor.

Paul Burst of the Claridge knows as much about card counters as anyone. He should; he has been battling them for years. Here is what he has to say to those who want to be card counters:

"Unless the counter is going to devote almost full-time to preparing himself and then putting his skills to use, he is better off keeping a perspective. And that is that card counting, or any skill he gains as a blackjack player, will give him a better game. He will last longer, and probably win more often, but he won't get rich at it."

Occasionally a Las Vegas casino will even tease counters by advertising single-deck blackjack on its marquee. "This is just a novelty to get people in the door," says Dunes floorman Earl Brookner. If a counter starts increasing his bets, "the casino will use the same method of breaking the deck, and the counter will find it is no better than playing against a shoe."

Indeed. With all the primers on how to win at blackjack, even with all the strategems on counting cards and splitting aces, the casinos don't seem to be too worried. To date, there are far more blackjack games than any other table games in the hotels. Does that tell you anything?

Worst bet at blackjack? Splitting 10s. Why ruin one good hand to possibly wind up with two bad ones.

Best bet? Doubling down . . . when your first two cards total 10 or 11, and the dealer has a 5 or 6 showing. Gollehon says you should always play in a casino that offers "optimum playing conditions," such as the surrender rule and the choice of doubling down on *any* two cards. Remember, rules vary from one casino to the next.

TRIVIA: Decks of cards are changed at the end of each eight hour shift. Chips are made of a plexiglass blend, and cost around 45¢ a piece to manufacture. So if you want to take a $5 chip home with you as a souvenir, the casino will be happy to see them leave.

Race And Sports Books

With the popularity of sporting events soaring, due to expanded television coverage, Las Vegas sports books are enjoying unprecedented success these days. Many of them are handling around $40 million a year in business, and keeping between 2 and 5% of that money as their "hold," depending on the game.

How does the book make its money? When a sports bettor makes his wager on football or basketball he must lay $11 for every $10 he bets. If he wins his bet he gets the $11 back, plus the $10 he won; but if he loses he has forfeited his $11, and that extra dollar represents the house percentage of 5% (1/20).

The top draw at Vegas sports books are professional and

college football games. Players can bet against the "point-spread," taking or giving points depending on which team is favored; parlay and teaser bets, where the player can bet on from two to ten different contests; or bet the totals, where the player can bet "over" or "under" the total number of points scored by both teams. Irv Silverstein, a former Las Vegas sports book manager, defined teaser bets this way. "A teaser bet is exactly what it's called. And anyone who knows anything about sports wagers will stay away from the teaser." So much for that.

Baseball is the number two attraction in terms of betting popularity. Straight bets are based on "odds to 5," such as 6 to 5 or 7 to 5, and for some people are a bit more complicated than the easier point spread.

The third top crowd-pleaser is basketball, although the betting limit is not as high as it is on football and baseball. Other betting attractions are boxing, hockey and major golf tournaments. It's been said that the really "pro" players concentrate on basketball, both pro and college, and on college football. It's also said that what sports books lose on Saturday college football, they more than make up for on Sunday pro action. Apparently, the pros are less predictable. And you thought this book didn't have any "hot" tips!

Who makes the line for all those ball games and prize fights? Usually it's a consensus opinion by professional Las Vegas oddsmakers, and the line is sometimes adjusted after the first bets are made at the earliest-opening sports books. Injuries to players are taken into consideration, and—as the pros call it—the home team advantage.

The biggest event of the year for sports books is Ye Olde Super Bowl Extravaganza. Forty million dollars was wagered on Super Bowl XX in Las Vegas, but the books took a beating on a proposition bet involving William "The Refrigerator" Perry of the Chicago Bears. The sports book at Caesars Palace gave 12 to 1 odds that Perry wouldn't score a touchdown. He did, and the sheep ate the wolf. "We lost $120,000 on that one," said Caesars sports book manager Art Manteris, but he added that the hotel's winnings overall on the Super Bowl in 1986 was "significant, high. No, make that tremendous."

Then there's horse racing. Its popularity is "unreal," said Irv Silverstein, and he looks for this sport to "be a necessity in all books in the near future. People enjoy getting away from the tables and watching the live TV coverage of horse racing." Races are shown from twelve tracks around the country, and there's also harness track racing at night.

Worst bet at a Vegas sports book? Making a ten-team parlay. The odds of pulling this off are well over 1,000 to 1, and what do you get? Six hundred to 1! No thanks.

Best bet? A straight wager on one game, but shop around for the best line, especially on college football.

TRIVIA: The Gaming Control Board has ruled that by 1988 *all* sports books must use computers to record both bets and payoffs. "It's the easiest way to detect any possible wrongdoing," says Silverstein, "and gives hotel auditing a clearer picture with computer readouts." These computers will cost each Las Vegas sports book an estimated $200,000.

So there you have it, friends and neighbors. These are the basics of all the games in Las Vegas. From roulette to blackjack, craps to keno. And now it's time to present our "Golden Fleece" awards, given to the top stars in the casino. May we have the envelope, please.

Number one, in terms of the games people like the most, are the slot machines. Number two, blackjack. Craps is number three, and the others in order are video poker, keno and roulette. The rest of the games didn't even place in this survey prepared by the Las Vegas Convention and Visitors Authority.

How does that stack up with the games that give you the best odds for your gambling dollars? Not too good. Craps edges out baccarat, but barely, with blackjack (assuming average players) in third place. Rounding off the list are electronic slots, some bets in keno, and 25¢ slot machines that offer jumbo jackpots. Just remember, though, that when you plunk two bits in the quarter slots you're not winning a million dollars when the sign says "win a million." Look a little closer. "WIN A MILLION . . . quarters."

Think of gambling as what it was meant to be when it began, eons ago. A way to while away time when there was no such thing as television, or radio, or even books in some places. Entertainment, that's what it's really all about. In a sense, it is almost like being immortal for a couple of hours, of touching hands with people who lived and died a long long time ago. When Grecian soldiers would spin their shields on the points of their swords and then bet on where they would stop. When Caesar himself played on a chariot wheel in a gaming room of his palace. Even as you read this, people are gambling their lira and their francs on five of the world's continents.

So if you jet to Vegas expecting to lose a few dollars and have a lot of laughs, chances are you won't be disappointed. Not when you hear an avid blackjack player tell his friends, "It's easy to win; you just have to *be* the cards." Not when you see a furious floorman yank the dice off the craps table after six passes and *smell* them. Not when you watch a slots player put a solitary coin in the money tray before he starts playing . . . for "seed."

Not when you realize that when you buck the casino you're like David taking on Goliath, only the big guy's got the slingshot! Of course, the casinos can quote from the scriptures, too.

"Lo, he was a stranger, and we took him in."

CHAPTER 5

Superstition

The word SUPERSTITION is defined in the Funk & Wagnalls dictionary as "a belief founded on irrational feelings, especially of fear . . . a belief in omens, charms and signs."

Keeping that definition in mind picture the following scene: a Las Vegas casino; players three-deep around the craps table, hollering, shouting, screaming; spectators pushing in to see the action; stacks of chips everywhere. It's one of those seldom-seen gambling phenomena . . . a hot hand, a "freight train," the chance to finally get even or maybe even *win* something. The stickman pushes the dice to the shooter. He shakes them confidently, as the other players offer encouragement or wait expectantly with hope and trust and even *love* reflected on their faces. The shooter lets the dice go. One lands on a six and the other one—oh, *no!*—sails off the table. The players all groan, but then the shooter calls out, "SAME DICE!" And everyone relaxes. It's going to be okay.

But if the shooter hadn't asked for the same dice there would have been bedlam. "Take my bets down." "I'm off this roll." "No action on my numbers." After all, every gambler worth his salt is familiar with that old proverb:

Dice on the floor,
Seven at the door.

And here's another one that every dyed-in-the-wool dice player knows by heart:

Play with the dice,
And they get like ice.

So when a real pro is gambling at a craps table he will pick up the dice, maybe set them on the number he's trying to roll, and let 'em fly. Or he might toss one of the cubes up in the air a couple of inches, just for luck, and then throw them. But he won't toss them *both* in the air, because everybody knows that's bad luck.

Good luck. Bad luck. Where did it all come from? Is it Man's way of explaining the unexplainable? Or is it just human nature not to blame one's self for all life's misfortunes? It's so much easier, and sometimes downright logical, merely to chalk it all up to . . . "just my luck." But if something nice happens to somebody else, then it's a different story. He's lucky. He was born with a silver spoon in his mouth. He's got the luck of the Irish.

It's been said that if you had a nickel for everyone who wasn't superstitious, eventually you might have a dime. For instance, who among us has not crossed his fingers "just for luck."

This habit goes back to the Middle Ages and originally involved two people. The way it worked was the person wishing placed his index finger on the index finger of a well-wisher, forming a cross. Then the wisher wished while the well-wisher well-wished. After a while it got streamlined to the point where now the wisher can do it all solo, crossing his middle and index fingers and wishing his heart away.

Then there's three-on-a-match. The truth of this tale has never been established, but supposedly during the First War three soldiers lit up their cigarettes off a solitary match. It was at night, and an enemy sniper aimed his rifle at the tiny flame. When the third soldier leaned over the match the sniper fired. Who knows, it might have happened on a Friday the 13th.

Good luck is supposedly enhanced by wearing dirty clothes while gambling. It may not work, but it *is* guaranteed to win you a little extra room at the table.

If you're having a run of bad luck all you have to do to change it is twirl your chair around two or three times. Or gamble with borrowed money. That always works. But don't loan money to someone else while you're gambling. That never works. For really good luck go to church on Christmas night and take the first pieces of money laid on the altar. That means good luck for the whole year. Unless you get caught doing it. "Officer, I was going to put it back next Christmas, plus ten percent of all the money I won gambling."

For a guaranteed hot streak you may spit on the palms of your hands (politely, please); blow on the dice (lightly, please); squeeze the cards (slightly, please). But never lose your temper or you will lose your money. Never leave your wallet lying on the bed or your bankroll will "fall asleep."

Singing during the course of play is bad luck. And bad manners. Dropping your cards is a no-no, as is counting your winnings while at the table.

We all know about black cats crossing our path, and walking under ladders, and that famous old standby: "Step on a crack, break your mother-in-law's back." Or something like that.

But did you know that sitting on a handkerchief will bring you good fortune? It's true. Sitting on a square of any kind is an ancient sign of good fortune.

One man who always carried a rabbit's foot was Colonel E. R. Bradley. He's the one who owned "The Beach Club" in Palm Beach. He also owned four Kentucky Derby winners. There was "Behave Yourself" in 1921, "Bubbling Over" in 1926, "Burgoo King" in 1932 and "Brokers Tip" in 1933. Anything unusual about those names? Nothing, except they all started with the letter "B," which was the Colonel's "lucky letter."

Bradley also believed that luck came in threes. If one of his horses went lame he was certain something would happen to two others. The same superstition, more or less, applies to famous celebrities. Their deaths are deemed to come in threes.

The old joke goes that it's bad luck to be superstitious, but sometimes it is difficult not to get swept away when the cards just aren't going right. So you don't pick up your hand until the dealer finishes distributing the cards. It's unlucky. So is letting somebody stand over you and peer at what you've got.

Many horse gamblers will never look at their tickets after they've bought them, and they'll never change their mind once they have finally picked a horse. Some will never bet on a white horse; others will never bet a filly against a gelding or a mare.

Poker players? Don't pick up your cards with your left hand. Don't let anybody put his foot on your chair. Keep your chips in a neat pile. It's good luck. But never gamble with your legs crossed.

Many gamblers believe they can "cheat luck" by changing tables, or dealers. Or: "Give me some new dice, these are worn out." A Las Vegas blackjack dealer remembers a player who suddenly pushed all of his five-dollar chips in front of her. "I thought he wanted change," said Debra

Phillips of the Dunes. "But he said, 'No, no, I just wanted different chips. I wanted some lucky ones.' It's the first time I saw that happen, and I've been dealing seven years."

There was a player who frequented the Mint in Las Vegas, a level-headed businessman who owned three corporations. "He was one of the nicest guys you'd ever meet," said another dealer. "Except if you'd say 'Good luck, sir' when you gave him his chips, his face would go white and he'd holler 'What? What did you say?' And he'd grab his money and run out the door."

Many gamblers don't consider themselves superstitious at all, but they will wear a lucky hat, or a lucky sweater, or lucky shoes, or lucky jewelry. Just in case. One woman would come to the Dunes Hotel with lucky *rosary beads*, each bead a small dice complete with little numbers on it.

It's all because people are superstitious. Especially gamblers. But wait! There is another group of people even *more* superstitious than gamblers . . . the people who *run* gambling places.

When Lady Luck blows a goodbye kiss to the casino boss and starts flirting with the customers—watch out. Okay, so it's not uncommon to change the cards when a player has a run of good luck. That's understandable. So is taking the dice off a craps game if they "get out of line." But then it begins to get a bit ridiculous. (Remember, we're talking about grown men here, some with even high school educations.)

Dice in some casinos are placed in what is called a "penalty box," where they sit forlornly until a pit boss decides that they have mended their ways and are ready for another chance in life.

If the dice were cold, a boss in one casino would wrap

them up with such notations as "you can use these dice to-day; they were very good last night."

A casino floorman in one Las Vegas hotel was sent home because he wore white shoes to work, not knowing that the shift boss had an aversion to them. Seems a player wearing white loafers beat the place out of a few thousand dollars the month before.

One supervisor would make his dealers drink ice water before going on a game that was losing money. Another would talk to players during a hot hand, the idea being to break their concentration. One boss would drop chicken bones under the table if things really got bad. His reasoning was . . . "Well, it was bad luck for the chicken, wasn't it?"

Did you ever see someone spill salt on the table? What's the first thing they do after they say "oops"? Why, they throw more salt over their shoulder! Nothing wrong with that; it's to ward off evil spirits. But in Las Vegas, salt was used by one pit boss to ward off evil *winners*. From Mike Goodman's book, "Your Best Bet":

"The boss of one big Strip hotel keeps a salt shaker in the desk in the crap pit. When the dice start passing, he grabs the salt shaker, walks over to the shooter, and sprinkles salt all around him. This boss has been doing this for years and the only result has been a dirty carpet."

This story has been verified by a Las Vegas dealer, who said sometimes the boss would get so carried away he'd have to order more salt shakers from the coffee shop. "He poured so much salt on one poor devil," the dealer laughed, "that when he walked away he looked like a miniature snowstorm."

One former dealer tells about the time he was taken off the dice game after a big roll. He thought he had done something terrible as the pit boss screamed at him, "I saw what you did. You did it right in front of me! What do you think I am . . . stupid?" "What did I do?" swallowed the dealer. "What did you *do?*" You called that winner! *Right in front of me!*"

It seems that in order to become a successful pit boss in the gambling business you have to sincerely believe there is such a thing as lucky dealers, and unlucky dealers. Years ago, at the El Cortez in downtown Las Vegas, one boss handicapped his help, just like race horses.

"In the old days," said one Vegas veteran, "certain dealers were picked out as hot stickmen, who were bad luck for the joint. They would never fire them, but they wouldn't allow them on the front games on weekends."

One floorman had a unique way of getting the dice to stop passing. He would jingle his car keys at the stickman, his way of "breaking the spell." Another boss would balance himself on one leg like a flamingo until the dice missed out.

There was a dice table at the Fremont Hotel that showed a sure and steady profit, month in and month out. That table killed every living human being who came near it. Then one day rain began to fall outside, and in Las Vegas rain is front-page news in the local papers. But as it rained that day a leak developed in the ceiling of the Fremont directly over the head of one of the dealers on that very lucrative dice table. Rusty little drops of rain water started to slowly drip down onto the left shoulder of the dealer's crisp white shirt. So he suggested to the pit boss that perhaps the dice table could be moved a foot or two. "Are you crazy?" the pit boss roared. "This table is lucky, right where it is!"

Well, it makes sense, doesn't it? If Table One in the dice

pit is losing money, and Table Four is making money, any idiot knows what to do. Just move Table One over to where Table Four is, and move Table Four up to where Table One is, or was. And then they'll both make money. Moving a table for any other reason is just plain dumb.

At one casino on the Las Vegas Strip the entire twenty-one (or blackjack) pit exchanged places with the dice pit, a move that cost thousands of dollars—while the hotel was going through bankruptcy—and required shifting twelve twenty-one tables, a roulette table, a Big Six wheel and seven craps tables. The reason? You guessed it, the twenty-one pit was making money and the dice pit wasn't. But then after the big move was completed the bosses found to their dismay that the bottom line hadn't changed. The twenty-one pit was still making money, and the dice pit was still in the red.

Ladies and gentlemen, we'd like you to meet Squatty. At least, that's what his friends called him. He was one of those superstitious pit bosses, and he's probably still wishing on a star somewhere. Squatty couldn't stand it if the dice began to "parade" on a game. When that would happen, and the shooter was rolling winner after winner, Squatty would slip up and vigorously rub the dice together on the two fives. Why? To bring on a loser seven, what else! Or if that didn't work he would tell the stickman to knock the dice around, so that the dice would "forget" what the point was.

One boss actually took the dice off a game after a big hand and *burned* them, because they had the misfortune of landing with the wrong dots pointed up. The dealers on the game might have been burned at the stake, too, if there hadn't been a law against it at the time.

Here's another true story, believe it or not. A blackjack

floorman was fired from one Vegas casino for having his left foot resting on a stool while the rack of chips on the table slowly went south. And as the pit boss wrote out the floorman's termination slip he told him "When you want winners you put your *right* foot up. Any fool knows that."

This floorman was a typical American white-collar worker, with a wife and a house and a couple of kids . . . suddenly out of work because he had the wrong foot on his stool! Thank God that foot wasn't encased in a white *shoe*, or he might still be looking for another job.

An ex-dealer at Circus Circus relates the following tale: "I was on this dice game when a big hand showed, and the pit boss was standing next to me muttering under his breath, 'I need a seven, I need a seven.' There wasn't much happening on my end of the table, so I closed my eyes, like I was really concentrating. And, sure enough, the next roll was a loser seven. The boss looked at me like I was some kind of *angel*.

"Well, a couple of nights later this same pit boss came running up to me in the pit and said, 'I need you on Table Three. The dice are really spittin' down there.' 'What do you want me to do?' I said, because I had already half-forgotten about that other incident. And the boss said, 'I want you to get me a seven.' I told him, 'I'm sorry, boss, not tonight. I've got a headache.'"

Stories like this make the superstitions of ordinary people look like kid stuff. Did you ever watch other gamblers when a new player sits down at the table? Most of them will automatically lower their bets, as if to say, "Well, there goes the neighborhood." One card player, who suddenly sailed into choppy seas, claimed it was because the casino was pumping more oxygen into the atmosphere. "Oxygen, oxygen!" he cried. "Who turned on the oxygen?!"

If the dealer's luck went sour, the boss was ready with a reason. "Did you get to bed before nine o'clock last night?" he would ask the dealer. After all, if a person doesn't get enough rest it's a lot easier for bad luck to slip up on him.

One dealer who worked in New Orleans during the war said that gamblers would be thrown out of his club for such infractions as smoking a pipe, eating peanuts or carrying an umbrella. A Chinaman once walked into the horse parlor of the club with an umbrella tucked under his arm, and instantly every race went off the board.

A former dealer said there was a popular superstition in Ohio, where he worked in an illegal casino. "If the porter was sweeping the floor, and you accidentally got hit by the broom, you were going to go broke. One morning there was a big poker game going on, when one of the players started screaming. The cards went on the floor . . . all the players stuffed their money in their pockets . . . and everyone headed for the door in a mad rush. You'd have thought a bomb had gone off! But it was almost just as bad. The porter had bumped somebody with his broom handle.''

CHAPTER 6

Casino Bosses

The most important person in the day-to-day operation of a gambling resort is the casino manager. He is on call twenty-four hours a day, and is the liaison between the general manager or president of the hotel and his subordinates in the casino.

His office is usually on the ground floor of the hotel, with a secretary in the outer waiting room to handle a never-ending stream of telephone calls and visitors. But what does a casino manager *do* all day? Said one: "There is more of doing nothing as a casino manager than there is of doing something. Our authority is delegated to shift bosses and shift supervisors." Another said, "We're all paper tigers now. Due to the influx of corporations, everything has to be done in memo form. To tell you the truth, I'd be lost without my secretary."

What it all boils down to is having qualified personnel in key positions, and sometimes having the wrong person in the wrong job can bring a casino manager's whole world tumbling down. "I made a grave error at my last job," one said. "I had a very good administrative aide. The man was excellent at what he did. But what I didn't know was that he was hated by the employees. Consequently, the employees lost respect for me. And I had no idea of what was happening until it was too late.''

Most casino managers arrive at work between 9 and 10 o'clock in the morning. The first order of business is to read the daily profit-and-loss statement to find out how much money was won . . . or lost . . . the preceding day. If the casino lost money, there might be a memo from the general manager requesting additional information. For example, one of the blackjack tables is in a prime location. Because of this it might show less of a win "percentage," but it will "earn" much more money than the other blackjack games in the casino. Suddenly, the earnings change, less money is being played on the table, and it becomes the casino manager's responsibility to find out why.

'I spend a lot of my time investigating,'' said one casino manager. "I work to find out why some of the games aren't showing the profit they should. Sometimes I'll do it myself; sometimes I'll use an outside agent. He'll play the game as a customer, then make a report to me.''

Casino managers, as a rule, are secretive about their work routines. So what we have done is mapped out a sample day in the life of a casino manager, based on interviews with former and present casino executives.

9:30 a.m. Park company car in private parking space.

9:35 a.m. Enter office.

9:40 a.m. Study profit-and-loss statement, read memos.

9:55 a.m. Return telephone calls. (Every casino manager receives at least a dozen calls a day from people looking for jobs—dealers, boxmen, floormen. "It's one of the biggest problems there is,'' one casino manager said ruefully.)

High rollers from out of town will also want to talk with the casino manager. They will want to make reservations to stay in the hotel, with as many "comps" as they can get . . . and although this is usually delegated to casino "hosts," many big players demand personal service from the "top brass."

10:45 a.m. Leave office on way to Staff Meeting, scheduled for eleven o'clock in general manager's conference room. Stop in dice pit and check with pit supervisor on morning's action. A player named Mr. Z has won $40,000, but still has a marker for almost $300,000. Mr. Z has been coming to the hotel for years, and will sometimes stand at the dice table for 24 hours at a time. That is, he *used* to stand at the table; now he sits at a stool and plays. Rumor has it that he lost the circulation in his legs from standing at the gaming tables for such extended periods. Now, in ill health and with a disposition to match, he is still a valued player and receives special treatment. He is allowed to play "on the rim," which means his markers are kept in the dice pit and not sent to the cashier's cage or fed into the computers like other markers. He will normally pay his gambling bill when it nears one million dollars.

11:00 a.m. Staff Meeting in conference room. Among those in attendance, seated randomly around conference table, will be: General Manager at the head of the table, Casino Manager, Assistant Casino Manager, Food and Beverage Director, Vice President of Hotel Operations, or the Hotel Manager, Security Manager, Chief Engineer, Advertising and Promotional Director, and the Purchasing Agent. There will also be a secretary present to record the meeting. Questions expected to arise at the Staff Meeting have already been prepared by the general manager's office and distributed to each department head, so there should be no surprises.

The meeting drags on for two hours. The general manager is upset with a statement made by Colorado Governor Richard Lamm, which has received broad coverage in the local newspapers. "One out of every eight women in Nevada is a prostitute," Lamm has been quoted as saying. Once again Las Vegas is finding itself smeared as "Sin City." The general manager asks for opinions on how to get the Colorado governor to retract his statement, and it is decided that the general manager will telephone the local Chamber of Commerce.

Another hot topic that gets plenty of comment is the upcoming golf tournament that the hotel is sponsoring. The GM wants to know why the casino block of rooms is tight. He's heard rumors that the hotel did not set aside enough rooms to handle the expected influx of big "shooters." And he wants answers.

"The hotel manager didn't honor our block number," says the casino boss. A heated debate ensues, and the casino manager jumps out of his seat, "Forget the no-shows, we simply don't have enough rooms. Where the hell are we going to put them?"

The GM is alarmed and wants a list of the high rollers that have made reservations through the casino. He sets up a private meeting with the hotel manager for later in the day. This guy has been on the proverbial "hot-seat" before.

It's the promotion director's turn to report on the success of his media campaign for the televised event. The GM listens. The food and beverage director confirms that he has laid plans for additional help and overtime to serve the weekend's "full house." Maintenance has everything in tip-top shape. The GM continues to listen. But there's no question he's concerned about the rooms.

The casino boss wants to get in another punch. He claims there are reports of rude treatment to his best customers at the front desk. He names names and wants the employees transferred away from his customers. He brings up an old problem about long lines at the reservations desk and again asks for a VIP check-in service that he feels strongly about. He lists all the other hotels that have incorporated this service and tells the GM, "Look, you know that the first impression at the front desk is important. These guys want to check in quickly, hit the room, shower, and get to the tables. Why the hell are we jerking them around!" The GM starts to answer but the casino boss interrupts, "They expect preferential treatment, and we give it to them every place else!"

To the casino manager's delight, the GM wants a report from engineering on setting up a VIP area, and asks for additional comments. There's no response. The hotel manager and his assistant are still smarting from the earlier accusations and are fearful of the meeting the GM wants later that day.

Other matters on this particular agenda include discussions about invitations to be sent out to more high rollers for the July Blackjack Tournament only four months away. The GM wants the information before the end of the week from the casino manager, who's on the hook because the tournament last year didn't turn out so well. The prize money had been reduced because there weren't enough players to justify the advertised jackpots. And the GM remembers, all too well.

"Geez," says the casino boss, "we haven't even had our golf tournament yet and you're concerned about the blackjack thing. These guys have to make plans and fly in here, you know. They don't live here!"

The GM doesn't answer the casino manager's complaint, and instead reiterates that he wants everyone on the mailing list with a $2,000 card and up. End of discussion. Now, it's the promotional director's turn to talk, but the casino boss is thinking about all the work he has to do and where the glory will go if the tournament is a success. As the publicity specialist talks, the casino boss tunes him out.

The last item on the schedule could easily become another shouting match. The GM wants a report on costs from engineering and maintenance on moving the casino around again, this time to make way for a new slot machine carousel that the casino boss is not happy about.

The boss interrupts, "How many blackjack tables are we going to lose this time? Christ! My casino's going to become a damn slot arcade!" The GM doesn't think it's funny. They both know that slots give the casino a big profit, but there's a serious clash in philosophy, and it shows in this heated discussion. A decision is made to present a new floor-plan in one week, to be approved at the next meeting. Purchasing has already been instructed to order the new machines, and the publicity director has his layouts ready to show. "Very nice," says the GM, "now what about the marque? We really have to promote this thing. The president wants to see those babies humming, and soon!"

The casino boss just shakes his head. Another frustration. Another headache. The new school beats the old school, again.

Meeting adjourned.

1:05 p.m. Casino Manager enters coffee shop for late lunch at his private booth in the corner. Sometimes he will eat alone, but often he will combine lunch with a business appointment. "Anything unusual ever happen at lunch?" we asked one casino manager. "As a matter of fact, I once noticed a long line of people waiting to get into the coffee shop, and a lot of dirty tables. I called the hostess over and asked her about it, and she told me that two of the busboys had gotten into a fight. I told her to get me a busboy jacket, and for the next forty-five minutes I cleaned tables.''

2:00 p.m. Stop in dice pit and tell the floormen about the lousy staff meeting. The casino manager is not only the casino's connection to the "upstairs" offices, he's also in charge of the gossip grapevine. Everyone wants to know what went on.

2:20 p.m. Answers page. It's his wife and he has another chance to tell his version of what went on at the staff meeting.

2:30 p.m. Stop in "21" pit and tell the floormen about the lousy staff meeting. But it seems they already know. The *assistant* casino manager had already stopped by.

2:35 p.m. Another page. This time it's a new casino host who wants to "OK" a room-comp for a player that he's really not that familiar with but wants to help. The casino manager tells the host the casino's policy on comps for the umpteenth time. "Look, tell him we'll make a decision on his room rate *at the end of his stay*. Hell, I can't get involved with this type of player. What's he got, a grand?" The casino host says he promised a casino-rate on the room, and he'd appreciate some backing on it. The casino boss is getting frustrated. He knows the new host came from a dust-joint downtown. "When are you going to learn the way we do things up here, for God's sake. This is a class hotel! We don't *give* things away!"

2:40 p.m. Return to office to read mail. Dictate memos to secretary regarding Staff Meeting.

One: Details on new credit procedures; copies to General Manager, Assistant Casino Manager, Credit Manager, Shift Bosses.

Two: Clarification of salary dispute. A backup pit boss who had worked in the capacity of pit boss several days before should be paid the same salary as the man whose job he had done. Copies to Payroll, the Blackjack Pit, and original to Backup Pit Boss.

Three: Reiteration of company policy concerning Sheriff's cards. In answer to complaint by State Gaming Control Board, all casino personnel must have Sheriff's cards in their possession while on hotel property; a spot check earlier in the week revealed that many workers did not have their work cards with them. Copies to General Manager, Assistant Casino Manager, Shift Bosses and Time Office where memo will be posted.

3:00 p.m. Return telephone calls. Several casino managers from other hotels want character references on prospective employees. Call Casino Manager at Maxim Hotel, who is a personal friend—weekend business warrants an extra dice game, but there are no "pucks" to mark the point during play. The last time this happened the casino used *ashtrays* for this purpose, which rather destroys the image of pomp and grandeur that Las Vegas strives to maintain.

4:45 p.m. Leave office.

8:30 p.m. Back to work, this time through a dark and deserted outer office. There is a telephone call almost immediately; the shift boss is with an irate customer who has lost his $10,000 in credit and demands an additional $5,000. Players who lose large sums of money while gambling require equally large doses of tact and diplomacy. "People get delirious when they're losing," a casino manager said. "I remember being in the dice pit one night when a floorman told me a very funny story. I'm standing there laughing, and this player who had just lost a large bet on the table happened to see me—and he thought I was laughing at *him*. I had to be escorted to my car by security!"

8:40 p.m. Turn on TV monitors in private office. The two black-and-white screens can be tuned to any game in the casino, by pushing corresponding buttons on the sets. Several players have complained recently about rude employees, and by watching the TV monitors of live action in the casino it can be determined whether or not these accusations are true.

9:15 p.m. Study monthly Hotel Report, prepared by the Auditing Department. Dictate several ideas for future casino marketing, to be incorporated into presentation at next Staff Meeting.

10:00 p.m. Review rating slips of current players in hotel. Rating slips are important because they tell exactly how each gambler plays: the length of time he is at the table, his average bet, whether he won or lost. Of course, a rating slip is only as good as the information received. It is the responsibility of the casino floormen to evaluate players, and sometimes—because of all their other tasks—the rating slips will be done hurriedly and inaccurately. It is not uncommon for a player to receive a "good" rating on the next game with an average bet of $200, and a "poor" rating on the next game with an average bet of $20. It really depends on how busy each floorman is, and how much time he has to rate individual players.

Rating slips have also become one of the latest scams in Las Vegas. A former casino manager uncovered a plot recently by a hotel host working with a casino floorman. The host was bringing small-time players into the hotel and giving them excellent ratings, signing the floorman's name to each. Consequently, these players were getting full complimentaries during their stay in the hotel. The host was getting a hefty percentage based on all this pie-in-the-sky (not to be confused with Eye-in-the-sky), and the floorman was getting a kickback from both the host *and* the players. And guess what the hotel was getting? It's spelled s-h-a-f-t.

10:30 p.m. Return telephone call of casino manager at hotel downtown, a friend for many years. The conversation is about a mutual acquaintance who was a casino manager at another downtown resort. This man had been at home on his day off celebrating Mother's Day with his family, including his mother who had flown into town for the occasion. The president of the hotel called just as the family was leaving the house for church services. "I need to see you right away," the president told him. "Steve," chided the casino manager, "do you know what day it is?" Assured that the meeting was not important, the casino manager spent the day with his mom. The following morning, when he returned to work, he found out he had been fired.

10:50 p.m. Walk through casino, stopping half a dozen times to chat with hotel visitors. Check the play in both the dice and blackjack pits. Find out how the games are doing by talking to supervisors. If there have been big winners, find out who they were and talk to the floormen who were watching at the time.

11:35 p.m. Leave hotel. It is that rare moment when the casino manager is alone with his thoughts. All the rewards and all the recognition don't mean much when you limp home bonetired every night—the free car, the credit card and the airline card, the hefty salary and the bonuses, the "power of the pen." That may have been mightier than the sword in the old days, but a casino manager can get the sword, too, at any given time. He works six days a week, sometimes seven. He hasn't spent a day with his family since his vacation last October. Maybe his wife will still be up when he gets home. Maybe they can just sit and talk like they used to. "How are the kids? What birthday?" Maybe they can take the telephone off the hook just once. But they don't dare.

The great majority of casino managers earn their pay. But for many, it's easy to delegate their responsibilities to the assistants. In fact, some assistant casino managers claim they do virtually all the manager's work. During a recent strike in Las Vegas by the culinary union, a casino manager at a top "strip" hotel asked his assistant manager to put in a little extra time. That "little extra time" turned out to be 78 straight days at ten to twelve hours each day, without a single day off!

The assistant casino manager is sometimes a shift boss also, and works the busiest shift from 10:00 a.m. to . . . whenever. In some cases, casino managers have been known to earn over $150,000 a year; the assistant casino manager might make $50,000 or $75,000 if he's lucky. Which job would *you* rather have?

Whether you're a casino manager, assistant casino manager, shift boss, or even a pit boss, the fevered frenzy to attract high rolling gamblers results in a lot of job turnover in Las Vegas gambling halls. One casino boss, who has had three different employers in the last three years, once said jokingly that he would forget which hotel driveway to turn into when he reported to work in the morning. He is Jeff Silver, former Chief Operating Officer of the Landmark, former Chairman of the Board at the Riviera, formerly a vice-president at Caesars Palace. "It's a system not unlike professional sports where once your troth is pledged to Bum Phillips, chances are you should rent your apartment on a month-to-month basis."

He found that working with so-called gambling experts

wasn't all he thought it would be. As a matter of fact, from his thousand days in the gaming business he came up with a new definition of the word "expert." Silver said, "An expert is a man who knows 500 ways to make love but can't find a girlfriend."

But he also said that for all its faults the gaming industry is "a most exciting and lucrative calling. Once you have had the taste, little can compare."

But casino workers know all about the "domino theory." New owners hire new presidents who hire new casino managers, who bring in their own little armada of shift bosses, pit bosses, floormen, and dealers who they play golf with. And out goes the old armada, to search for another battleship. One floorman was so insecure from all of this that he lived in a motel room with a hotplate, because he didn't know how long he would be working. Yes, there's nothing like Las Vegas—meeting new people all the time. Like that cute secretary at the unemployment office. Whenever one of these battle-scarred warriors fills out a new job application, it's an all-day affair listing every spot he's worked in the last ten years. One pit boss got around all that, though. "Hell, I just put down 'various hotels.' "

Sometimes, if a guy has been out of work long enough, he'll try to repay the favor when a casino finally hires him. The casino manager of one Strip hotel noticed on his daily "P-and-L" sheet that the "Big Six" wheel showed a win percentage of 100%. Something like $625 was bet on the game that day, and the casino won every single bit of it. The next day it was the same story; the "big six" held 100%. Ditto the following day. The casino manager decided to investigate, concealing himself behind a row of slot machines to watch the recently-employed dealer in action. The dealer would check to see where the bets were on the table, then slow the spinning wheel with his hidden hand so that nobody ever won anything! The boss called the dealer into his office and demanded an explanation. "Heck," the dealer said. "You guys done all right by me. It was my way of saying thanks."

Meanwhile, new bosses keep coming and going at each hotel, which sends the maintenance men hopping. Early in 1986 Richard Bunker quit at the Dunes to go to the Aladdin. Burton Cohen, who had been in charge at the Desert Inn, replaced Bunker. John Alderfer, who took Cohen's place at the Desert Inn, apparently didn't like Cohen's old floor plan, so he revamped everything at the Desert Inn. And Cohen thought Bunker's layout of the Dunes was all wrong, so he started moving the casino around to the way things were when he was at the Desert Inn. But while Cohen was doing this, Bunker was busy fixing up the Aladdin so it looked like the Dunes when he was over there.

All this gets pretty confusing to the average tourist, who comes to town maybe once a year, and confusing to the maintenance men who have to do all this. Said one as he wiped his brow, "It seems that every time the hotel gets a new manager we have to start changing things. We just finished moving a row of slot machines from one spot in the casino to another. Would you believe we're getting ready to move the lounge further away from the casino? It's going to be a new area for more slot machines. It'll cost over $30,000. But that's what they want. They're the experts . . . I think."

And speaking of "experts," most old-line casino bosses share the common view of the new-wave, corporate managers. Memos come down from upstairs in language that the casino bosses can't understand. Words like "profit conversion ratio," "linear programming," "corporate asset pooling," "balanced income adjustment," and "coefficient of cash-flow variations."

What the hell do these words mean! A CPA we contacted was able to define only one of these crazy phrases. According to him, "Corporate asset pooling is a method of accounting for a business combination under which the assets of the acquired firm are subsequently carried on the merged firm's books at the same value that they were carried by the selling firm."

Right!

A retired casino boss who had recently faced this dilemma, commented in no uncertain terms. "This all stems from the corporations that came to town. These guys can relate to their businesses in other areas of the country, but not gambling. It's like a company that manufactures thumbtacks. The bosses know how many thumbtacks are going to be spit out every year from "projected inventory" or "some such mumbo jumbo, and how many households are going to buy the things. So they try to follow the same procedure in the gambling game."

What happens is that the casinos find themselves in a "Catch 22" situation. Since each department is on its own, people get laid off when profits drop. Consequently, service goes down. Service goes down and customers are lost. Customers are lost and profits go down. Profits go down and more people are laid off. And the whole cycle repeats itself. As one pit boss said, "Someday someone will get smart and rediscover the casino, which is what this business is all about anyway."

Said another, "It's like I told 'em when they came to Caesars. 'You college boys want to run these places like a

J.C. Penney's. But a gambling joint is . . . a gambling joint.' ''

Since the whole casino industry is based on "house percentages" and "true odds" and all the other statistical data, you would think that the bosses know all of that stuff by heart. Do they? "Some do, most don't," said a Summa vice-president. The real experts are the mathematicians and the unknown enemies-of-mankind who devised and developed these casino games in the first place, a long time before there was such a place as Las Vegas. The floormen you see behind the tables are really there for one reason, and it's not to compute odds and probabilities. Robert Harrington: "It's mainly their job just to see that everything runs smoothly, that there is no form of collusion going on, and that the customers are satisfied.''

That's what it all comes down to—keeping the customers happy so that they, in turn, will keep coming back. If one hotel starts getting more business than the rest, the others will send someone over to find out how they're doing it, so they can do it too.

Bob Brooker of the Marina remembers when the blackjack dealers at Caesars Palace stopped looking at their hole-cards. Up until then, dealers always checked their bottom card when they had an ace or 10-value card face-up.* "I went down and looked at it a couple of times, and discussed it with my casino manager.'' Not only did the Marina follow suit, but now "it's fairly standard up and down the street.''

A Las Vegas casino can't just change its gaming policy at the drop of a hat. If a hotel wants to switch from single

---

*The theory behind the change is to prevent the dealer from signaling the value of the hole-card to a player working in collusion with the dealer to cheat the casino.

odds to double odds on the dice tables, or from double odds back to single odds, or anything else that is different from what it has been doing, it has to notify the Nevada Gaming Commission. Another job for the busy casino manager.

We'll end this chapter with a well-known "boss story." A blackjack dealer at a big "strip" hotel needed $200 in a hurry. He went to the casino manager and said, "Listen, I gotta have two hundred right away, it's an emergency." The boss said, "I'm gonna give it to you this time, but next time you need money you do what the other dealers do . . . steal it off the tables!"

CHAPTER 7

Comps And Credit

Casinos try every trick in the book to keep the players with the big cash coming "home." To do that, they use amateur psychologists . . . baby sitters . . . diplomats . . . and referees. Only their official title is none of those. They're called "hosts." Every resort hotel in Las Vegas has one, two, five or ten of them.

When a VIP checks in, he doesn't have to go through the regular line with the hordes of others waiting to register. He has a special window so he doesn't have to wait. The hotel host is notified immediately and will hurry over to welcome this special guest and help him carry his wallet to his room. If he's with his wife, she gets a rose or a carnation pinned to her blouse. Naturally. And when they get to their suite of rooms their favorite liquors will be stocked. Naturally. If it's their anniversary, there will be a little gift on the table. It's all part of the ceremony, and that's what being a host is all about.

"I make people feel like a big shot." Gene Kilroy, casino host at the Tropicana.

"Everybody wants to be somebody when they come here, and I help 'em feel like somebody." Mitzi Gobel of the Frontier.

"My job is to make customers feel happy and excited." Mark Winer, director of VIP services at the Las Vegas Hilton.

"A host romances the customers." Ash Resnick, host at the Dunes in early 1986.

Sometimes, being on a first-name basis with a big player means being on a first-name basis with a new boss. Resnick introduced one of his premium pals, Ginji Yasuda of Japan, to Aladdin Hotel owner Ed Torres. The result was that Yasuda, who had a yen for a Vegas property all his own, bought the Aladdin for $54 million. That means Resnick will be following Yasuda to the Aladdin, where former Dunes chief Richard Bunker is already entrenched. But the estimated $12 million in business that Resnick brought to the Dunes is just another example of how important hosts really are. "Knowing people, bringing them in, knowing how much credit to give and knowing how to collect the money. That's what it's all about," Resnick said.

Mitzi Gobel, the second woman ever to be a host in Las Vegas, said a female host "has to be tough like a man, feminine like a lady, and work like a dog." It's like running a nursery for people over the age of 40, according to Ms. Gobel. "If they lose, we listen to 'em whine. If they win, we listen to 'em gloat."

Each casino host in Las Vegas sends out about 3,000 invitations a month. The gold-embossed cards are high quality and say things like: "Hi—I would like to treat you to my style of Old Fashioned Las Vegas Hospitality—Call me." There's a toll free number under the host's signature.

Sounds simple enough, until you figure that a hotel like the Frontier . . . with ten hosts . . . each sending out 3,000 invites a month . . . 3,000 x 10 x 22¢ postage . . . or $6,600 per thirty days before anybody even shows up!

One host, who claimed to have 50,000 names in his current file of customers, said he spends extra money out of his own pocket to have all his invitations addresssed by hand. "And I always write 'personal' on the envelope. That way, I know they're going to open it."

As far as figuring out what kind of "comps" to give to individual players, the formula varies from one casino to the next. But, as a host explained, "it's usually fairly simple. If a player stays at the table for five hours a day, and his minimum bet is $25, we'll give him a special room rate. If he plays for five hours and his minimum bet is $75, we'll give him a free room. Five hours with bets of $100, and he gets RF&B (room, food and beverage). Anything over that, and we'll throw in his air fare." Or maybe even the air*plane.*

A player doesn't necessarily have to stay at the tables for five hours. Take a player with a $5,000 card (credit line).* Robert Harrington, former Tropicana casino manager, says he would tell this player, "If you can show me that you have the opportunity to try to win $5,000 from the casino, and that the casino has the opportunity to win $5,000 from *you,* then you'll be given all the complimentaries that you want."

It's common knowledge that gamblers who have a lot of money can be expected to lose a lot of money. Dishing out a thousand dollars worth of comps to an oil tycoon who has lost 50 times that much in the casino is just good business. Good business for the casino; bad business for the oil tycoon. Besides, the hotel can chalk it all off on its taxes, while the oil tycoon thinks he is getting away with

---

*A credit line is set up on a scale of how much money is kept in a player's checking account, since there is no way of finding out about other financial holdings such as savings, stocks and bonds. So if a man has a $5,000 card it means he has at least $5,000 in the bank when he gets to Vegas.

something. But what he's getting is a $10 bottle of champagne that the hotel sells for $30 that cost the hotel $6 because it buys the stuff in bulk. And when you consider what the oil tycoon lost on the tables, it's probably costing him $500. And he's happy!

It's like the old man who told his offspring, "There are a lot of things that are free in this town, but son, you can't afford them."

High rollers expect all these perks and freebies, and they know that if they don't get the red carpet in one hotel they will get it in another. There was one who called a floorman over and said, "My wife and I want to eat in the gourmet restaurant tonight. Take care of it, will you?" The floorman made all the necessary arrangements. "You're all set, Mister B. Seven o'clock tonight." The high roller, whose eyes never left the dice table, said, "Okay, now call my wife in the room and tell her to get ready."

A host said that it's not uncommon to have over a thousand dollars worth of charges made to room service each day, just from the suite of one big player. One woman ate so much cracked crab on ice—when she first got to her room—that she was bedridden for the rest of her stay in the hotel. The "do not disturb" sign which hung from her doorknob probably saved the hotel a fortune.

Back in the days when junkets were big business, wine would be ordered by the crate from room service. After the junket players checked out, maids would find no bottles in the rooms. It was obvious what was going on. The people were taking the booze home with them. A scream of outrage was heard when the waiters started opening the bottles before taking them upstairs. Then there's the old story about the junket player who complained about the towels in his room. They were so fluffy that he couldn't get them in his suitcase.

Junkets seem to be slowly receding into the Las Vegas history books. The costs just simply don't warrant the action—chartering airliners to bring them to town, chartering buses to get them to the hotel, wining them, dining them, giving them all the choice rooms, throwing big parties for them when they arrive, throwing bigger parties for them when they leave. It has turned out to be a losing proposition for everyone but the people on the junkets. And the casinos don't like it when *they* have to pay the markers.

That's one reason casino hosts are so vital to the gambling industry, a sort of last link with "civilized man." The way Gene Kilroy puts it is, "The dice and the cards are the same all over. It's how you treat people that makes the difference."

Frontier host Babe Schwartz says, "I've made a lot of very close friends—and I don't mean acquaintances—and I've never let a man go beyond his means, because you can wash out a lot of people that way. I still try to trust people like the old days, and I don't look into a computer for answers."

Kilroy, Schwartz and Resnick all have something in common, something besides being hosts. At one time or another they were all connected with professional sports, and high rollers—for some reason—like to associate with sports figures. That's why big boxing matches in Vegas fill up the town. Gene Kilroy at the Tropicana is a former business manager for Muhammad Ali. Resnick was a top basketball star years ago. Anyone who knows anything about baseball knows that Babe was a great shortstop for the Chicago White Sox.

Then there are the "celebrity" hosts. They don't really *do* anything. But they're famous, and that's all that counts. Johnny Weismuller of "Tarzan" fame was first. And then there was Joe Louis.

According to a spokesman at Caesars Palace, "The concept behind that was that Joe Louis was one of the most famous people in the whole world. Caesars got him for a nominal amount of money, and he just hung around the casino day and night. To most people it was like shaking hands with President Reagan."

No matter how much money a fellow had, or how many businesses he ran, it was still a kick to go back home and brag a little bit to his friends. "I was talkin' to Louis over at Caesars in Las Vegas. You know, *Joe* Louis? The brown bomber?" Or, "That Johnny Weismuller, what a crazy guy. Want to hear what he told me over at Caesars in Las Vegas?" Or, "Man, am I tired. I've been playin' tennis for the last three days. With Pancho Gonzales. Over at Caesars in Las Vegas."

Pancho Gonzales? *The* Pancho Gonzales?

Si, señor. Pancho, one of the all-time greats of professional tennis, can still bat that little ball back and forth with the best of them. He won the U.S. championship two years in a row at Forest Hills, and went in the record books when he won the longest match ever played at Wimbledon in 1969. Today he is the tennis pro at Caesars. If a high roller goes up to the boss at Caesars and says, "I want to play tennis with Pancho Gonzales," the boss makes a phone call and the match is set up.

It's the same story in Atlantic City. Want to talk baseball? The Claridge Hotel now has Mickey Mantle on its payroll. His official title is "host" but his unofficial title is "former New York Yankees baseball star." Named the

Most Valuable Player for three years during his career, Mantle also holds World Series records for most runs (42), most runs batted in (40), and most home runs (18) in total series games. He's not hitting on baseballs now; he's hitting on high rollers. It's like Robert Harrington said. "I'm sure a lot of people would be intrigued even to see Mickey Mantle." But they can only see him at the Claridge.

Over at Bally's Park Place, there's Willie Mays. He and Mantle are both in the Baseball Hall of Fame, and Mays got there by banging 660 homers and making impossible catches out in center field until his hat fell off. And Mays got to Bally's Park Place by being a celebrity.

Baseball Commissioner Bowie Kuhn huffed and he puffed when these two former athletes went to Atlantic City in 1980. Then he tried to blow the house down. These two former players were giving baseball a bad name, he said in so many words, by their association with gambling. Until they "mended their ways" they were divorced from baseball. But Kuhn got *himself* divorced from baseball, and a new commissioner rescinded the ban.

Now Mays is back with the San Francisco Giants, teaching others how to touch bases. And he's still touching bases with Bally. "Hey, now," he said in a recent interview. "I wanted to be back, but I wasn't gonna beg. I think I've always felt I should be out on the field." Being suspended for six years, just for trying to make a living, was painful for Willie.

Baseball may always be America's number one sport, but lifting that ban against Mickey Mantle and Willie Mays proves something else. Gambling is becoming another accepted American sport. No one will say how much money Mantle gets for rubbing shoulders with the masses, or how much Willie Mays makes for saying "say hey" until his voice cracks. But an insider at Caesars Palace said Joe Louis received between $40,000 to $50,000 a year.

For *regular* hosts, who have to work for a living, salaries vary from $25,000 a year at the very low end of the scale to $500,000 a year. Most of the old-time hosts get around $75,000 a year, according to Dennis Gomes of the Las Vegas Hilton. But, he said, "I know of one host who has a $250,000 salary and $200,000 in expense money."

The casino host's job doesn't end when the big shooter arrives at the hotel, as we've pointed out. But just seeing the player through his stay at the hotel isn't the end of it either. Someone has to watch the player at the tables, and someone has to "rate" the player, to make sure he's keeping up with his end of the bargain. The casino would not take lightly to a high roller who sucked up all his comps, while spending most of his time on the golf course, in the spa, or on the tennis courts.

All players with a credit line are evaluated by a casino floorman. And we mean "evaluated." A casino rating card, like the one shown, is used to record information about the player's successes (or failures) at the tables. "Time in" and "time out" means the length of time the player stays at the table. That's a critical factor for the casino since they know that they have the advantage over long-term play. A few short-term wins never phase the casino bosses, because they know that the longer a player stays at the tables, the greater the likelihood that the player will lose.

Exposure. That's what it's all about. The few players who know how to "hit and run" are not the casino's first choice. They like the players who grind it out. Their term for this type of player is "casino-oriented." But a more accurate term for them is "loser."

"Game speed" is not so much the speed of the player,

CASINO RATING CARD

Date: _____

Name: _____

Game: _____ Table #: _____

TIME IN: _____ AM ____ PM ____

TIME OUT: _____ AM ____ PM ____

CREDIT LIMIT: _____

REQUESTED: _____

AVERAGE BETS

Start _____ End _____

GAME SPEED

Fast _____ Average _____ Slow _____

Player: _____ _____ _____
            win   lose   walk

TOTAL HOURS PLAYED: _____

FINAL EARNINGS: _____

Floorman's Initials: _____

Preliminary Rating: 1 2 3 4 5 6

Shift Boss Initials: _____

Final Rating: **1 2 3 4 5 6**

but the speed of the *game* while the player is at the table. If the table is full, then the game is slow. If the player is facing a blackjack dealer "head-on" (no other players at the table), then the speed is fast. "Speed" means decisions. The more decisions per hour, the faster the player will lose his money. Remember, the casino has the edge on every toss of the dice, every flip of the cards, and every spin of the wheel. Assuming our high roller is not a skilled card-counter, and for all intents and purposes he isn't (few are), the faster the game, the faster he loses.

Decisions. Decisions. That's what the house wants. If our high roller is fumbling with the dice, the floorman might tell him to "pick 'em up and shoot 'em.'' Players who "play" with the dice are slowing up the game—and slowing up the casino's profits! At the blackjack tables, dealing six or eight decks from a shoe increases the number of decisions per hour, by cutting down on the time when a dealer is shuffling—a time when the casino isn't making any money! When you have the odds in your favor, as the casino always has, speed is a most important criterion. That's why it appears boldly on the casino's rating card.

Of course, the size of the high roller's wagers are important too. Perhaps most important of all. The floorman "licks his chops" when he sees a player come out with $100 chips, or even a stack of $25 chips. Big bets! That's what the casino wants. And if that's what the casino wants, would you suppose it's best for the casino or for the player? Most players will never learn that the smart bets are the small bets. **Making small bets when you begin playing, then increasing your bets as you continue to win is the mark of a tough player.** You're reinvesting your profits as any smart businessman would do. And the smart player has enough sense to get out when the table turns against him.

Gaming author John Gollehon said in his book *Pay the Line* that "the smart gambler lets the casino take his small bets, then hits them over the head with his big ones. He starts small until he's ahead. No gambler in his right mind begins play with big bets."

But tell this to the high rollers.

So the casino is looking for players who begin play with big bets. But we're on *your* side, not the casino's. We hope you don't!

Remember, increase the size of your bets only when you're well ahead, and especially when you're riding a long streak of winning hands. Like Gollehon said, "Hit 'em over the head!" That's probably the best advice you're going to get in this book. Better advice would be to "stay out of casinos!" But that's not what you want to hear.

Surprisingly, the final tabulation of your outcome, win or lose, is not that big a factor in determining the extent of your comps. If you gave the casino a good shot at your money, yet you won, that's great! The casino won't take your comps away. Indeed, they'll want you back at the tables soon, so they can have another shot at you. Sooner or later, they'll get you.

If you're one of the very few players who keep records of all your winnings and losses over the course of several years, you know that it's a virtual certainty you're on the short end of the stick. But few players keep track. Every trip to Las Vegas wipes the slate clean.

Incidentally, if you think you can write a marker at one table, then leave that table, or even that pit, and go play at another without the floorman aware of you . . . guess again. The casinos have it all figured out. There's solid communications between the pits, even the twenty-one and craps pits are tied together. That's what the phones are for!

"Rudy, see that guy in the blue shirt, he just walked up to table three. Let me know how he does. He's down five hundred over here and should have about eight black checks with him. And watch him closely . . . he has a habit of sneaking checks in his pocket. Thinks he's cute!"

The floorman will pass the card along to the shift boss when the player calls it a night. It's up to the shift boss to give the player a final rating. "6" means a tent in the parking lot, but a "1" gives the player in question a free run of the hotel. It's like being in Tiffany's with somebody else's Visa card. Meals, drinks, room, health club, golf course, tennis courts, shows—all free, and in some cases even airfare for two, first-class!

The rating system works effectively in most casinos, but sometimes there's a dispute, not between player and casino, but between shift boss and host. The host, as you recall, is not responsible for the rating, but *is* responsible for the player. A bad rating can hurt the player's chances for future comps, and sometimes the casino host forgets whose side he's really on. The most frequent discussions between hosts and shift bosses are about ratings and comp considerations.

A heated debate usually ends up on appeal in the casino manager's office. Not only does the casino manager have the final say, he's expected to review ratings and comp totals for big customers anyhow, for the protection of the casino.

As you can see, the casino host is involved in the player's "action" from when the player checks in to when he checks out. The host wants to know the final score. How did his player do? Not what the player said he did, but what the casino people said he did. The only games you can play with these characters are at the tables. If you won, tell the host you won. He knows it anyhow.

Earlier, when we mentioned "credit-play" and "writing

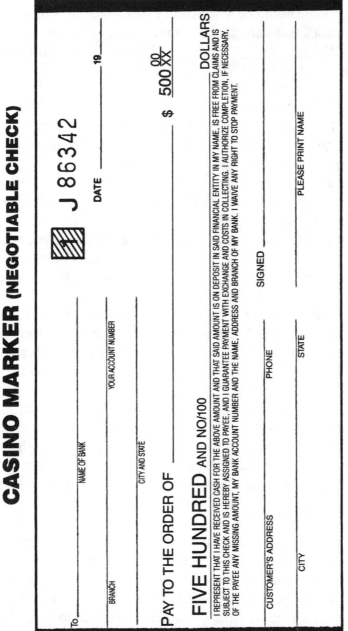

markers" it should be made clear exactly what this involves. Applying for credit, as we pointed out, is not much different than applying for credit at a department store. But *using* credit in the casino is a little different story. Casinos don't use charge cards . . . at least not yet. What they use today are called "markers," which few players realize are actually checks . . . real checks that can be deposited at your bank for payment like any other check. Our illustration points this out clearly. Read the fine print.

Credit in a casino is not really a credit account. What the casino is really doing for you is giving you "check-writing privileges."

The practice of writing markers is certainly not reserved for high rollers. Just about anyone with decent credit can receive a credit-line and write markers. The problem comes with the simplicity of it all.

"I really should quit. I'm out of money. Ah, what the hell, give me another thousand." It's so easy. And so dangerous! If you're reckless with your credit-cards back home, credit in the casino is a bad, make that *very* bad idea. Give it serious thought before you apply.

It should be pointed out that the main purpose of writing markers in the casino is not for the player's convenience, and certainly not for "status," but for the player's hope of acquiring comps. Without the credit-play system, the casino cannot monitor your play in anticipation of any comp considerations. That's why most players write markers. Because they're expecting a comp. They give the casino a reckless shot at a *few thousand*, for a chance to "win" a *few hundred* in comps. Does it make sense?

That rare player who is indeed a professional gambler doesn't play for comps, he plays for cash . . . the casino's cash! To him, comps and credit are a joke. Besides, to play on credit he would have to give the casino his vital stats . . . and that's the last thing he wants. You'll usually find him at the single-deck blackjack tables . . . making modest-size bets. And nobody knows who he is. Don't confuse "professionals" and "high rollers." They're two different breeds.

For those of you who are not high rollers—or professionals, for that matter—getting a room *without a reservation*, even a room that you expect to pay for, can be a real headache . . . especially on weekends. Don't believe for a second that there is such a thing as a completely booked Las Vegas hotel, no matter what Bambi at the front desk tells you. Hotels follow the same procedure as the major airlines; they overbook their accommodations to guard themselves against "no-shows." Then in case everyone *does* show up Bambi starts her prepared little speech by saying there was a—quote—computer mistake-unquote. And that is all—quote—hogwash—unquote.

They don't know that you now know what they all know . . . that there *are* rooms in the hotel reserved by the casino for its special players. These are the players who turn up unannounced, and the hotel keeps rooms for them, just to be on the safe side. This is called the "casino block." The casino also has "blocks" of seats in the showroom set aside for its cream-of-the-crop gamblers.

All you have to do to get a room, even when the hotel is filled, and all you have to do to see a show, even when the theater is sold out, is stroll casually to the cashier's cage and set up a credit-line for a few thousand dollars. But do this during the day so the casino can call your bank! Then mention to somebody in charge that "I'd love to gamble a while, but—darn—my wife and I don't have a room here, and she's been dying to see Wayne Newton. We usually stay at the Hilton, but then my stockbroker told me about your hotel . . ."

You'll get a room.

Something else you can beat are the long, winding lines waiting to file into the Las Vegas showrooms twice a night. Is there a way of getting past that line, even if you are not a so-called high roller? You bet! We asked former casino manager Robert Harrington. "I wouldn't hesitate to give anyone a 'line-pass,' but the majority of people are afraid to ask." Here is what you do. *Limp* over to the dice pit, or the blackjack pit, and catch the hungry eye of one of those fellows in the gray pinstripes behind the tables. "Excuse me," you say, "but my wife and I have reservations for the show tonight. Is there any way you could give us a line-pass? My wife's not feeling well, and I've got this bum leg I picked up in Korea . . ."

With the line-pass in hand, you and your wife can walk right into the showroom, like all the big muck-a-mucks do. When you get to the maitre d's station, tell him you want to sit "ringside." Tell him you'll "take care of the captain." That's the guy who actually seats you. When the captain gives you a seat you like, *then* tip him. Not before. It's hard to repossess tips!

CHAPTER 8

The Player

Many surveys have been undertaken through the years to determine why people gamble. They show that men gamble more than women, whites more than blacks, Jews more than Protestants . . . but poor people don't gamble more than rich people, and there is no evidence that gambling destroys the family. In fact, the idea is that gambling "is a pleasurable form of recreation and an escape from a humdrum existence," according to O. Newman in his book *"Gambling, Hazard and Reward."*

High rollers demand the most service. Southerners drink the most. Easterners are the most likely to lose their tempers when they lose their money. The novice player will usually say "thank you" once he is finished. Orientals are the most courteous, and seldom show emotion whether they are winning or losing. Women tip less than men. Celebrities tip less than women, and are—as most dealers will tell you—a pain in the neck. But they will bring a crowd to the table in less than a minute. Everyone wants to go back home and say they saw a movie star in Vegas.

A New York survey has estimated that 81 percent of the city's population gambled—33 percent of them on cards,

24 percent on numbers, 74 percent on lotteries, 36 percent on sports and 22 percent on bingo.

No one knows for sure how many of these people who bet the nags or the numbers or get down on the Yankees or try to fill an inside straight are compulsive gamblers, but there are ten million of them out there, according to Gamblers Anonymous. That's a staggering figure when you consider it breaks down to about one in every 20 Americans.

Modern theorists say that the compulsive gambler is like an alcoholic or drug addict, that with this type of gambler there is no such thing as moderation. At the Vegas chapter of Gamblers Anonymous, a volunteer worker and ex-gambler confirmed that compulsive gambling is an emotional disorder, "a very destructive one that bars no social stratum, no age group, no ethnic class." He went on to say that most suicides in Nevada, even among teens, had some association with this disease.

"They are not getting enough out of life," says Las Vegas psychiatrist Irving Katz. "They feel powerless. In gambling they have a sense of power. It gives them a feeling that they are somewhat controlling their lives and luck is on their side."

Las Vegas gambling bosses are certainly not psychiatrists, but they do see thousands of people a year bellied up to the tables. With the thought in mind that here we're talking about why the *normal* person gambles (if there is such a thing) let's get their opinions:

"Gambling is something that'll never change," one boss reflects. "It's just something that I can't explain. It's like kids. 'I'll bet you this,' 'I'll bet you that.' They start right in there when they're three, four years old. And if you had any idea of how much money was bet every day, illegally, with no taxes paid, it is astronomical. Astronomical. Why, they could cut out the national debt in one year!"

A younger casino floorman made this observation:

"It starts out as a game because everyone needs a game. And they lose. And now it's a challenge to their ego. We're talking about people here who are very successful in their fields . . . doctors, lawyers. With all the monetary rewards and plaudits, and things like that. And they keep trying to beat that game until they run out of money."

Maybe there's more truth than humor to the story of comedian Shecky Greene, who once leaped bodily into a crowded dice table at the Riviera and—as he slid down the layout—he bellowed at the startled dealers, "IT ALL GOES!"

Computers are now being used to estimate how much money certain gamblers will lose based on their type of play and the actual odds of the various games. The casino keeps an extensive file on most credit players, and of course they know all about their own games.

Say, for example that Herman Highpockets of Dallas is coming to the hotel for the weekend. Mr. H. likes to play blackjack at a thousand dollars a hand and he has $50,000 on deposit in the cashier's cage. He takes insurance when the dealer has an ace showing, he splits tens, and he always stands on "16." All this information, and much more, is fed into the computer, along with the fact that he's going to be "comped" for dinner in the gourmet restaurant and see Dean Martin in the showroom Saturday night.

Back comes a report something like this. "H. will lose approx. 20 percent of $50,000 because of house p.c., and 22.75 percent of remaining $40,000 because of said gambling techniques for house profit of $20,825, less write-off on comps of $1,200."

So poor Herman is flying in to Vegas with fifty thousand. He's going to eat lobster and cherries jubilee, watch Dino sing "That's Amore," and dump almost twenty big ones on the tables, and he doesn't even know it. The casino is going to chalk up a profit of $19,625 . . . and the casino *does* know it because the computer said so. And it better darn well turn out that way or there's apt to be a new floorman watching the twenty-one games on Monday morning. They are certainly not going to fire the computer.

One thing that doesn't register with the computers, though, is human error. "Dealers make mistakes, just like anybody else," one pit boss explained. "Computers don't figure things like that, or that the cards are going to turn against the house sometimes."

And what about poor Herman? He's not interested in the computers, or the people who run them. All he wants to do is play cards and have fun. If Herman doesn't feel right at home, down in the casino, he'll just walk across the street, to another casino. After all, everybody loves Herman.

It would seem that the "personal touch" of Las Vegas has gone the way of the steam locomotive, which is how the town got started in the first place. That time of gratuitous pampering belongs to an age when movie stars were sticking their feet in wet concrete at Graumann's Chinese Theater in Hollywood, when the man on the moon was always Buster Crabbe and not some upstart by the name of Armstrong.

It was a time when radio was dying and jets started flying, when the genuine heroes of American folklore had names that rolled off the tongue with a nice easy click . . . Joe Louis, Mickey Mantle, Willie Mays.

In Las Vegas, it was the era of the high roller, a happy and carefree moment in its history when the casino mogul could look down from his penthouse in the sky at all he had created and say, "Hey, dis is okay."

But then came the United States cavalry, with new orders from Washington. "Thou shalt not launder money." It is better known as Regulation 6A of the Department of the Treasury, and what it means is that any cash transaction in excess of $10,000 must be reported. This regulation is similar to Title 31 of the Bank Secrecy Act (which all casinos in Atlantic City follow), and Title 26 that requires businesses to report cash outlays of over $10,000.

Exactly what is laundered money? Here is an example. A person goes into a Las Vegas casino with a large sum of cash which he can't show as income from any legal enterprise. He exchanges the cash for chips, then makes three or four bets on the tables. After that he goes to the casino cage, where he trades the chips for a cashier's check. Now he can say, "Well, I won the money gambling."

The casino is also a great place to launder "street-money." It's easy to change a stash of $5, $10, or $20 bills into $50's and $100's. All those "dirty" wadded-up $5's and $10's become "clean" C-notes, and a lot easier to store or spend. Maybe hundred-dollar bills are not that popular back home in Pleasantville, Ohio, but in Las Vegas they're standard issue. Put another way, nobody in Las Vegas will be impressed when you hand them a hundred-dollar bill, even at McDonalds.

With Regulation 6A, any time the total of a player's cash transaction within a 24-hour period exceeds $10,000 he must provide the casino with his name . . . permanent address . . . and driver's license . . . or passport . . . or other suitable ID.

Said one supervisor at Caesars Palace, "Since that regulation came out, I know five or six high rollers—legitimate businessmen—who haven't played here. They've got to give their name, and social security number? Listen, only a *fool* would do that."

This regulation, according to California law professor I. Nelson Rose, is "costly, confusing and frightening to both casinos and players." A survey he undertook showed that large casinos are filing an average of 40 reports a month, while 60 hours a month are spent processing the paperwork. The result has been a 25 percent drop in business for Nevada race and sports books while the casinos have lost 10 percent, Rose said.

But even before this, the high roller was becoming an endangered species. After all, how much oil can be pumped out of an oil well? How much gold can be dug out of a gold mine? How much coal can be chipped from the side of a mountain before it finally topples over?

It's like the true story of the high roller who loved to gamble. Loved to gamble? Even *that* was an understatement. He played in Vegas for thirty years, and was recognized at every casino on the Strip. "Mister G! How are you? Welcome back."

Mr. G was the chairman of the board of a large corporation back East, and when he raised one finger as he approached the tables it didn't mean there was a bird overhead. It meant: "Give me ten thousand." This was in the 1950s. By the sixties one finger in the air meant: "Give me one thousand." And in the 1970s five fingers meant: "Five hundred." He died shortly after that, a victim of his one great vice. Ironically, that finger which once meant a thousand . . . no, ten thousand dollars . . . was used a final time—to pull the trigger of Mr. G's own revolver.

Of course, there are other less painful ways of escaping this damsel of distress . . . running when you win, and running when you lose.

There was a man from Phoenix, who sold franchises to make his fortune. When he was in Las Vegas he would stay at the tables until he couldn't get another dollar on credit. With his wallet running on "empty" he'd head for some other casino where he had more credit to "fill up" with. Once he won $16,000 playing blackjack at the Stardust, but it burned the proverbial "hole" in his pocket. He took the money two blocks down the Strip to the Flamingo and ran it into memories. But on his last trip to Vegas somebody in heaven fell in love with this Phoenix gambler. He went to the Flamingo, with ten thousand dollars, and won. He went to Caesars Palace, and won. He went downtown to Binion's Horseshoe, and won. And won. In four days of dice and cards he amassed over a million dollars—1.2 million, to be exact. He was never seen in Las Vegas again.

Then there was the extremely wealthy doctor from San Francisco. Actually, he started out as extremely wealthy, but when Las Vegas got through with him he was just . . . rich. He was well-known in this one particular casino, where he could call out his bets to his heart's delight and then settle up later. But there always come a time to pay the piper, and it arrived one wintry afternoon for our California doctor. "Young man," he said to the floorman, "how much do I owe?" The floorman looked the doctor straight in the eye and answered, "One hundred and ninety-eight thousand, four hundred and sixty-eight dollars, doctor."

The doctor blinked. "How much?" he said again. "One hundred and ninety-eight thousand, four hundred and sixty-eight dollars," the floorman repeated.

"That is a good deal of money," the doctor managed after a short pause. "And—I—don't—have it!" With that the doctor made a bee-line for the front door of the casino.

There was apparently a rash of emergency appendectomies in the Bay Area shortly after this incident, because two weeks later a check arrived at the casino from the doctor's office in San Francisco. It was for the amount of $198,468.

A Texas oilman lost $320,000 during an all-night session at a Strip casino. The next night he won it back, only to lose it again the following night. The fourth night he won it all back again. All this was too much for the owner of the hotel. He had him thrown out of the place. "Get out!" he was supposed to have told him. "And take your $320,000 with you!"

In another Las Vegas casino every boss in the joint would come running when this certain player showed up at the craps table. It all seemed rather strange to the other spectators, because the man would only bet one-dollar chips. What the spectators didn't know was that the gambler getting all this attention was under the constant surveillance of the Internal Revenue Service. What the IRS didn't know was that each of those one-dollar chips was really worth three *thousand* dollars!

Along that same line, another high roller in one hotel didn't like having a crowd around when he was playing, so the casino gave him black chips with the $100-inserts removed. Each of these chips was worth a thousand dollars. This player caught a big hand on the craps table one day and walked away with over $200,000. Before leaving, however, he gave the woman shooting the dice three of his "special" chips. The casino got some of its losses back right away, when the pit boss told the woman, "Let me give you some real chips for those, lady." And he gave her three $100 chips. She was thrilled, not realizing that she had been shorted by $2,700. Probably to this day she is still telling her friends about the time a player gave her three hundred dollars in Vegas.

There was a couple from Oklahoma staying at the Mint Hotel in downtown Las Vegas. Lady Luck not only smiled at them; she gave them a toothy grin. They couldn't believe it. When they cashed in their chips they had over twelve thousand dollars! The husband got so excited that he called his boss in Oklahoma and quit his job. Then he headed right back to the tables. To make a long story short, he wound up blowing the whole twelve grand. And there he stood, a dazed, vacant, and "unemployed" expression on his face. His wife was looking straight up into those dazzling chandeliers overhead, and wailing to all within earshot, "He LOST it, he LOST it. . . "

They only lost $12,000. Ten years ago at the Sands, a Stardust cocktail waitress won—and then lost—$280,000. Her game was blackjack. She knew when to hit and when to stand; she knew when to double-down and when to split pairs. But she didn't know when to split the scene. At one point during her 24-hour marathon at the tables she deposited $100,000 in the cashier's cage. And then those cards—which had caressed her and fondled her—began to slap her and torment her. The chips in front of her slowly disappeared, and so did the other hundred thousand in the cage. The bosses at the Sands weren't sorry to see her lose, but the dealers sure were. Each of them made $450 in "tokes" from her that day, while she walked away with nothing but a look of disbelief.

Or how about the skinny kid who walked up to a $5 blackjack game at another Strip casino. The next thing you know he was at the $25 game, and then he was at the $100 game. He had never had so much money in his life. He was betting big, and he was tipping big. He'd started with nothing but a $5 chip, and here he was with $160,000. Then—poof! It was all gone. Again, the only ones who came away the winners were the dealers. They scored $400 a piece. This story isn't over yet, though. After the kid lost all that loot he asked for a free room at the hotel. The pit boss told him, "Let the dealers get you a room. They can afford it." And so the dealers did. They all chipped in and got the kid a suite for the night. Like the cocktail waitress from the Stardust, he went out . . . but he went out in style.

Here's a story that took place over 20 years ago, but it bears repeating. Elvis Presley's manager was a notorious high roller, and a meal in Las Vegas once cost him a lot more than the price listed on the menu. Colonel Tom Parker had just finished dining in the gourmet restaurant at the Aladdin when he ran into owner Milton Prell. He remarked to Prell how good his turkey dinner was, and Prell told him to stick around. "I'll get you four more to take back to Palm Springs with you." The Colonel got the bird, all right. While waiting for Prell to come back from the kitchen he strolled into the casino. And by the time Prell returned, Parker had lost his appetite—and $100,000 in cash.

The trouble with most gamblers is that they just don't know when to quit. It all goes back to human nature. When they're winning they want to win more; when they're losing they want to win back what they lost. Then there's always some psychiatrist harping about "self-punishment"—that deep down inside, all these gamblers want to lose. Tell *that* to the Stardust cocktail waitress, or to the guy from Oklahoma who quit his job on the telephone. Maybe there are a few exceptions, but how many times have you seen someone lose his money and walk away from the tables with a big smile on his face?

Except maybe Mr. S. That's another thing. Casino personnel never call a player by his full name, only by his last initial. That way no one knows who he really is, which is how most high rollers like it. But Mr. S was a true lover of that gentleman's game called craps, and he always liked to stand right next to the stickman. He never said a word . . . he never smiled . . . he never even blinked! This man made Mount Rushmore look like a three-ring circus. He displayed no emotion whatsoever—until he started to win. Then he would begin blowing feverishly on his hands, his mouth twitched and trembled, and his eyebrows would start to hop up and down. Said a floorman who watched him play, "I've seen him win fifty, sixty thousand dollars on one shooter. Then he'll jump the opposite way and start betting *against* the shooter. When the hand is over he's liable to have lost $150,000!" Then Mr. S's eyebrows would settle down, his mouth would once again become a thin red line, and his hands returned to his sides. Somehow, Mr. S would seem at peace with himself again.

The man in our next tale is one of the richest people on the planet Earth. His income, without exaggeration, is over a million dollars a day. In Las Vegas his last name is "K" and his first name is "Mister." The hotels literally fight for this Eastern potentate's business, one going so far as to build a penthouse for him complete with a wood-decked hot tub and jacuzzi. Huge fans were then placed nearby and hotel porters, lined up like army ants, would bring pail after pail of ice cubes to be piled in front of these propeller-like devices. The result? A cool ocean breeze in the middle of the desert, for a billionaire who couldn't stand the Las Vegas summers.

Mr. K also liked to have two specific items in his hot tub with him: pretty girls, and rose petals. No problem. The girls were easy enough to come by, and he could order roses by the bunches from the hotel's flower shop. But one night when his secretary called the flower shop it was closed. The manager was tracked down in the hotel restaurant. "Open the flower shop," she was told. "Mister K wants more roses." The manager refused, saying she was off duty, but would fill his order in the morning. Needless to say, no more orders ever came from Mr. K's penthouse, which cost the flower shop untold thousands of dollars.

Mr. K had the usual entourage that rich and famous people seem to have. One night they all dined in regal splendor in one of the town's most famous gourmet restaurants. The very finest foods were prepared right at their table, and their every slurp and swallow was serenaded by violins. Afterwards, as they prepared to leave, Mr. K instructed his male secretary to leave a $3,000 tip. It was all Mr. K had on him at the time. The secretary waited until his boss left the room and then peeled off $500. The rest of the money went into the secretary's pocket.

When Mr. K gambled, he didn't shoot dice with the common riff-raff. He had his own casino, all roped and sealed off. There was a craps table inside it, and a roulette wheel, and a blackjack game . . . each with dealers standing by. They looked like German soldiers waiting for the invasion at Normandy. It was nothing for Mr. K to lose a million dollars at one sitting when he played, or to win a few hundred thousand. Of course, the bosses didn't get too upset when he won because he always stayed around long enough to lose *something*. His philosophy seemed to be, "They bought me dinner. The least I can do is make a few small wagers."

Here's an example of one of his "small" wagers. At the craps table he once bet $20,000 in the field; $3,000 on "any craps;" and $1,000 on twelve. (Before going any further, let's explain. "Twelve" is a one-roll proposition that pays 30 for 1; the "field" is a one-roll bet that pays 2 to 1 on aces or twelve; and "any craps" is another one-roll prop bet that pays 8 for 1.) Mr. K has $24,000 in action. Big deal. It would be like one of us commoners putting a dime in a pay telephone. The stacks of chips towered like miniature skyscrapers on that table. One of Mr. K's "sugar babes" had the dice, awaiting orders from her master. He nodded. Slightly. And with a "tee hee" and a "golly gee" she let them go. They bounced down the table and came to rest on a twelve! And in that one roll of the dice Mr. K won a total of $90,000. It all happened in less than a minute.

A cocktail waitress was serving him wine by the glass that day. When he hit that twelve for ninety thou he turned and dropped two $100 chips on her tray. But guess who came running? None other than Mr. K's male secretary. He grabbed the two chips and stuffed them in his pocket, and left her standing there dumbfounded. What was she going to do? She couldn't very well tap Mr. K on the shoulder and say, "Excuse me, but that *man* took those chips you gave me. Please, sir, could I have some more?"

There are many stories told about Joe E. Lewis, one of the greatest saloon comics in the history of show business. He was also one of the greatest gamblers to ever come down the turnpike. Once, when he was appearing at the old El

Rancho, he took his girlfriend out for dinner at a classy place on the Strip. Suddenly she ran out of cigarettes, so Lewis went out into the casino to get her another pack. He returned 20 minutes later, and they ate the rest of their meal in silence. Then, when they got up to leave, Joe noticed that the new pack of cigarettes was still on the table. "Hey, baby," he said, "don't forget your cigarettes. They cost me $32,000."

One of the weirdest players to hit town went by the nickname of the "Kingfish," according to a Caesars Palace pit boss. "He owned a string of fishing boats out in California. He used to call and reserve a dice table, and he'd bring 16 players with him." These players weren't friends of the Kingfish; they were people he hired for $50 an hour just so he could bet $34,000 instead of the regular per-player limit of $2,000. "He really thought he was doing something tricky, and he would orchestrate the whole thing. He signed the largest marker I've ever written. It was $367,000 for one afternoon's play."

Everyone knew when the Kingfish was in the hotel. On one of his first trips to Caesars he had presented the owners with a lighted full-color photograph, in gilded frame, of his first fishing boat. It was hung on a wall near the cashier's cage. When the Kingfish was back in California the light on the picture was off. When the Kingfish was in Las Vegas, the light was on.

These were the kind of players that came to town, once upon a time. There are still a few left, but Regulation 6A chased most of them away. Just before the 1986 Super Bowl one cash customer walked into a Vegas sports book, intent on making a $25,000 wager. Told that any amount over ten thousand necessitated the showing of some identification, he reduced the bet to $9,999.

Most players, namely the $2 and $5 bettors, are really not concerned about cashing out over ten grand! And until recently, most casinos were really not concerned about this level of player. But now the casinos have discovered this new group of players that it had never actively courted before: *the middle and working class.* Behind the tables these gamblers are known as grinders or low rollers for whom a few hundred dollars amounts to real money. Up until 1985 this type of player had been left to the smaller casinos, while the big resort hotels fought for the cashmere-clad high roller like "dogs fighting over a piece of meat," as one casino exec put it. But all that has changed. "We're targeting Middle America," stated Arthur Waltzman, president of the Riviera. The first thing the Riv did was open up a Burger King inside its plush hotel. Waltzman, an accountant by training, is just another example of that new breed of Las Vegas gaming executive, trained not as a casino pit boss but in more orthodox business endeavors . . . bringing his marketing skills to Vegas gambling properties.

The emphasis on drawing these middle-and-working-class gamblers to Las Vegas has spread everywhere in town. Aside from fast-food restaurants and lower prices on its rooms, some hotels have added recreation vehicle parks and low-stake slot machines that are swallowing up casino floor space and beginning to edge out table games.

"In years past, the high roller on table games was the premier gambler in Las Vegas," said Marv Leavitt, general manager of the Mint. "Now we've recognized that the dollar slot player can be worth more than a five-dollar table player." The Mint consequently set up a Silver Dollar Slot Club for regular slot machine players, sort of like a Rotary or a Lion's Club. The casino even sends these players personal cards on their birthdays and at Christmastime.

Hopefully the cards don't say anything like "Deck the slots with lots of silver, tra la la la la, la la la la."

Although the idea of courting Middle America is becoming a common theme in Las Vegas, not everyone believes the strategy will work. Says Jack Binion, president of the Horseshoe Casino:

"People are always talking about Middle America. I think that's a bunch of bull." Given the choice, Binion said, any casino would prefer a high roller. Even the low rollers themselves like to play among the big gamblers.

So what is happening is that many hotel executives in Las Vegas are trying to get *both*, by virtually dividing their casinos into low-ends and high-ends. That way, the small-time player won't be intimidated by valet parking or something in a tuxedo called a maitre d'. And the high roller won't notice the sports bettors gnawing on hamburgers and swilling beer out of Dixie cups.

The Dunes Hotel spent up to $30 million tacking on a whole new casino called "The Oasis," which was referred to by its employees as the "oh-anus." The minimum bet in that casino was one dollar, or a dollar and a coupon to win two dollars during special promotions. One female dice dealer remembers having scratches on her hands "from people grabbing at their money when I paid the pass line." But it attracted the low rollers off the sidewalk, which was what it was meant to do.

Caesars Palace made the move to broaden its audience in 1984. "We always had the top of the line, and still do," said Don Allison, president of the hotel. "But because we have two entrances, two casinos, 23 food and beverage outlets, we are able to look like several casinos and several hotels at the same time."

Caesars World Chairman Henry Gluck admits that in the early years Caesars concentrated on the premium-level play, "but we have made a conscious attempt to diversify and broaden the customer mix for all of our properties. And over the past couple of years we have been very successful. The customer mix has changed dramatically."

The Sands Hotel almost cast off its lifeboats in the early eighties. Employees were being let go left and right, and the Summa Corporation—which thought it had sold the hotel—suddenly had to take it back again. Its new president was Pat Cruzen. "To say we are fully recovered is not 100 percent truthful. But I think we're on the right track."

The big problem was that the previous operators dropped their attention to the average customer and went after the high-end guest. And now, says Cruzen, "our people have put together a marketing plan to attract both segments: the premium customer and the slot customer."

Unfortunately, when all the big casinos stop concentrating on the plump high rollers and start fishing for the lowly low rollers, it makes for empty nets for all the little casinos that have *always* sought out the low rollers.

Bob Brooker of the Marina gives more of an insight. "As things slow down everybody goes after the same business."

So the Marina has to offer the people something it can't get anywhere else. It does this by having its Special Events Department and its Casino Marketing Department dream up monthly extravaganzas to lure the low rollers back home.

"We have blackjack tournaments, craps tournaments, slot machine tournaments, video poker tournaments. Promotions are extremely important," Brooker says. "In the old days there were more gamblers than there were casinos; you just opened your doors and the people came in. But today it's not like that. You really have to promote to get the people in the hotel."

These promotions are also expensive. "They cost anywhere from twenty to fifty thousand dollars just to put on." And how much does the Marina get back? "Sometimes nothing. Our slot tournaments, for example, are set up so that we don't make any money. We'll actually lose a minimum of $10,000 per tournament. The concept is just to bring the people into our hotel, get them to know how friendly we are, and hopefully they will continue to come back."

Meanwhile, the Lady Luck Casino is spending $16 million on a *tower!* We're talking about the Lady Luck, not Caesars, not the Hilton, not the Bally Grand. If you haven't been to Las Vegas since 1946 then you probably remember it as "Honest John's Newsstand," where people would go on Sunday mornings to get the home-town newspaper. Now it's buying television sets for *two thousand* rooms!

It's downtown where the "real" Las Vegas always has been, in the minds of many seasoned players. It's home to the Horseshoe's "World Series of Poker," the Golden Nugget's "Grand Prix of Poker," the "Mint 400," and the Four Queens' "Golden Blackjack Classic." It's where the fireworks are seen from the top of the Union Plaza on New Year's, and televised nationally.

It's where the clatter of construction equipment competes with the clamor of the casinos; where Steve Wynn is spending *another* fifty million on his Golden Nugget, jacking up a 976-room skyscraper.

The Las Vegas Strip, still bloodied from battling Atlantic City, wearily pulls itself to its feet and calls for reinforcements. The lowly El Morocco (known as Elmo by its neighbors) announces plans to build a 19-story tower, the

Imperial Palace adds 800 rooms with a $40 million expansion, and the Flamingo Hilton spends $62 million reaching for the sky.

Circus Circus calls a news conference. Glenn Schaeffer, the hotel's chief financial officer, is at the microphone.

"There's been a realization in this town that yes, Middle America is the largest and most dependable segment of the gaming market. There just aren't a lot of people who can afford to lose a lot of money."

Circus Circus likes the low balls. Circus Circus never did want to blackball the low balls. Circus Circus caters to the low balls, and serves them highballs. Up to their eyeballs. And the world is beating a path to its door, family-style. Families, with annual incomes of under $50,000, appreciate Circus Circus, with the trapeze acts and the rubber-nosed clowns—and Wet'n Wild, the $15 million waterworks where the kids can play all day on the world's tallest water slide—and Ripley's Believe It Or Not Museum at the Four Queens, where you can see a man who ate trees and a man who ate scorpions. All most gamblers get to do is eat crow.

The new slogan in Las Vegas these days says it best. It's not catchy but it's cagey. *"Las Vegas . . . the American Way to Play."* It's almost unpatriotic *not* to want to go there. Now, $7.4 million is being spent beaming this message into every hamlet of the colonies.

A recent poll of first-class hotels around the world showed that double rooms with breakfast range from $150-to-$200 a day, New York topping the list at $210. In Las Vegas the Union Plaza charges $36-to-$50. A steak dinner with one vegetable and a potato costs $59 at Abu Dhabi and $42 in Tokyo. In Las Vegas dinner is $3.49 at Circus Circus.

Breakfast is 99 cents at the Bourbon Street, prime rib

and lobster is $7.77 at the Hacienda, beer goes for half a buck a glass just about anywhere and champagne is free "over at that little place next door to Circus Circus. Honest to God, Fred, you just help yourself." Of course, Fred has to go through the casino to get to the free champagne or the 99-cent breakfast, or the showroom. And maybe, just maybe, he'll get a little bored standing there in line, so he puts a few quarters in the slots, or plays a hand of twenty-one, or rolls the dice once, just to see what it's like. And they've got him. Fred is dead.

But nobody seems to mind, except maybe Fred when he discovers that the 99-cent plate of ham and eggs and cold hashbrowns he was after wound up costing him thirty or forty smackers. A woman will dig in her purse and come out with a wad of ones and fives, and a piece of paper with names and instructions written on it. "I'm making this bet for a friend of mine," she will announce, and when the money's gone she'll smile and walk away.

It all goes back to what a vice-president at the Sands told us. "For the most part, casinos carry all hotels."

Paul Rubeli put it even more bluntly. He is the man in charge of gaming for the Ramada Inns, which owns the Tropicana. "With the low-end players you're lucky to make 10 cents on the dollar, and the market for high rollers is too competitive these days. But right in the middle is that husband and wife who spend about $500. On them, we'll make 70 cents on the dollar."

It's all starting to fall into place. It seems there are THREE different categories of Las Vegas gamblers. . . the low roller, the high roller, and the *medium* roller. Maybe that's the reason why Las Vegas casinos are spending a total of $282 million on 5,117 extra rooms to bring the total number up to nearly 60,000. They can fight Atlantic City and the lotteries and each other at the same time. While the Strip is stealing downtown's low rollers and medium rollers, downtown is busy wooing the Strip's high rollers. You can have them, says the Strip, because there aren't many left.

To keep all those brand-new rooms filled with as many medium rollers as they can get, the hotels have had to put a lot more people on the payroll. As this goes to print there are some 76,300 Nevadans employed by Vegas resort hotels . . . or 17.6 percent of the state's total work force. And although some of the jobs don't seem as important as others, every man and every woman who punches a time clock in one of these supersonic structures has a vital role in keeping Las Vegas as American as apple pie. Most of the tasks are boring, and many workers are stuck away in rooms the size of jail cells that don't even have windows in them. But everyone is there for the same reason . . . to keep those dice dancing and those wheels whirling and those cards coming.

CHAPTER 9

Counting The Cash

A regular customer, who came to Las Vegas on the New York junket for 15 straight years, asked the dealer one day where the cashier's cage was. He wanted to cash in his chips. Asked the dealer, "You mean you've been coming here all these years and you don't know where the cashier's cage is?" The player answered, "I've never had an occasion to go there before."

How much money does a cashier's cage keep on hand, to cash checks and pay all its winners? Some hotels have over $1 million in the drawer . . . in cash! All resorts must keep a certain amount of money on hand, but not necessarily that much. It's based on the number of games in the casino and varies according to hotel size and day of the week . . . but for the average casino it is anywhere between $250,000 and a half-million dollars.

The casino cage is the center of all casino financial transactions. In fact, the "cage" gets involved even before some customers get to the hotel—by processing their credit applications and working with banks in their home towns to verify this information. Three different departments work inside the casino cage.

There's the Credit Department. Clerks in this section

keep up with the markers and payments of players with established credit. They also prepare the cage balance sheets, and maintain and update all player cards, including new accounts. Most Strip casinos have around 50,000 of these player cards in their active file. Let's say a new player walks up to a blackjack game and wants $500. "Have you been to the cage?" he will be asked. If he hasn't, then that's his next stop.

The cashiers want to verify that a player is indeed who he says he is. Next, the cashier will activate his records by putting this data in the computer system. It's a protection for both the casino *and* the player.

The cage itself is made up of a crew of cashiers, whose job is to service customers and the casino tables. They cash checks for hotel guests, swap chips for cash, set up the bankroll for the casino tables, and prepare "fills" for the games when more chips are needed.

Last, but not least, there is the Casino Collections Department. When a guest doesn't pay his marker before leaving the hotel he is sent an initial bill. If he doesn't pay it within 45 days he is contacted by telephone. Gambling losses at one time were not legally collectable, but a 1983 state law changed all of that. And now a gambler can wind up with his wages garnished, or even have a lien placed on his property. That law changed everything, and it was a long time coming—according to Dennis Gomes of the Hilton. He said:

"For Nevada not to consider them to be legal debts was to cast discredit on our business. The fact that they finally recognized gaming debts as *legal* debts was the final seal of approval on gambling as a legitimate business in the state of Nevada."

After all, gambling on credit is big business. It totaled

$1.83 billion in 1985 inside the state, and the casinos collected nearly all of it—$1.79 billion.

It is awe-inspiring to watch those casino cashiers at work, deftly whisking through stacks of bills a mile high, never losing their composure as they count to a thousand . . . to fifty thousand . . . to a hundred thousand, in cash! A hun—*hundred thousand*?

Then why aren't there any instances of robbers trying to knock these places off? We posed that question to Tony Foley, Assistant Cage Manager at Caesars Palace. "Caesars? Probably because it's so big, and there would be so many people to watch. The very openness of it all is its own security. Everything can be seen so easily. There's no place to hide. It's all in such plain view, and I think that very fact is what protects it."

Has anyone ever tried? "One time a guy came up to one of my cashiers and he gives her a note. 'This is a stick-up. I want five thousand dollars.' So she says, 'Wait a minute, I've got to get my supervisor.' Of course, Security grabbed the guy; he didn't have a gun or anything. And it turned out he was a mental patient. He'd done the same thing in San Bernardino two or three days before, only they gave him the money. This is the only time it ever happened at Caesars."

Have you ever looked closely at a casino chip? It doesn't look like money, it doesn't feel like money, but inside one of those Las Vegas hotels it *is* money. A $100 chip is worth $100, and if that chip is in circulation it means somebody paid $100 for it. But sometimes things can get a little sticky when it comes to getting those chips cashed. It's like the age-old story of paying car insurance for years on end and then trying to collect from the insurance company once you have an accident. They'll finally pay you, but you go through agony first. Case in point: A black man, shabbily dressed, betting two dollars at a pop on the craps table. He's shooting the dice. The point is ten. A high roller comes up to the other end of the table, and starts betting big money. The black man rolls winner ten. The high roller throws him a $1,000 chip. The black man goes to the cashier's cage to turn in the chip for cash. "Hey!" says the cashier, "where'd you *get* this?"

To make a long story short, the poor guy had a tough time convincing the cashier that he didn't steal it, which apparently was the casino's concern. He had the chip, but it took him a long time—and the aid of an attorney—to get his cash.

Black was certainly beautiful in this case, because the man not only got his $1,000—but he also won a discrimination suit which he filed against the hotel.

Sometimes chips from these casinos wind up in very strange places. Like church collection baskets. "We take a regular chip run every week from the Guardian Angel Shrine," said Foley. "But things have changed a little bit with these new federal regulations. You're supposed to cash your chips in each casino, and it's not quite as open as it used to be. But that doesn't seem to stop the churches."

Or chips will wind up in the bottom of some rich woman's purse, where her teenage son finds them. He goes to the cage, dressed in blue jeans and scruffy tennis shoes, holding on to a stack of chips worth $25,000. "Where'd you *get* these?" "Uhh, playin' back-a-rat." At last report the boy was still in the doghouse, and not allowed to use the Rolls on Saturday nights.

There are isolated cases where someone will complain about the casino's safety deposit boxes. "I had some chips in there and now they're gone." Or: "My grandmother's earrings are missing." Said Foley, "No chance! There's one key per safe deposit box, and the customer has it. If that key is lost, the box has to be drilled in front of three witnesses." The boxes originally come with two sets of keys, but "the second set is usually taken out and either dumped in Lake Mead or broken up by the head locksmith (of the hotel). So there's only one key left. And that's it."

Getting back to those casino cashiers, would it be a compliment to tell one she should be working in a regular place . . . like maybe a bank? "People have a misconception of what a cashier in a casino is. They think a casino cashier is like a dime store teller, or they'll say, 'Oh, you must have been a bank teller.' That, to me, is the highest insult. Because if we can't do the same work that three or four tellers do, in less time, we don't belong in the casino cage."

"We've got to be fast and accurate with large amounts of money, all the time. About fifty percent of our transactions are $5,000 and up." He said the busiest time of the year for the casino cage at Caesars "is during a fight weekend, when we'll handle hundreds of millions of dollars in business."

Of course, with all that money in the cage it gives crooks a lot of ideas. Foley, a one-time IRS agent, has tripped up quite a few. Once a man tried to cash a $350,000 cashier's check at Foley's window after the check had already been verified by Caesar's bank in New York. Foley had bad feelings about the whole thing and called the Philadelphia bank which had issued the check in the first place. "Yes, it's good," he was told right away. But still it didn't ring right, so he called the Philadelphia Police Department which sent a car to the address of the bank. It turned out to be a telephone answering service, in cahoots with the big-spender in Vegas.

Another time a Roberto Duran lookalike forged a $1,500 marker using the name of the former welterweight champion. But Foley refused to believe that the man was Duran and the fan took a van to the can.

"This goes on all the time," Foley said. "It's an ongoing thing; it never stops; it's a constant challenge." One of the biggest scams, he said, is "you sign my traveler's checks, I'll sign yours. We'll cash them at different casinos, then we'll report them stolen and get our money back." But people like Foley outbluff the bluffers and save Caesars Palace a ton of money in bad checks and stolen cashier's checks.

"This is what cashiering is all about," he summarized. "It's not just making change for a dollar bill. It's not just cashing a traveler's check. It's protecting the hotel against this kind of people. They try to outwit you, and you try to nail them."

"Nailing" is the responsibility of the casino's security department. This department is run like a miniature police force, which is exactly what it is. Only instead of a sheriff this squadron is under the leadership of a Security Manager, or "Chief" as his friends call him. The chain of command goes from him to the Captain (known as "Cap") to the Sergeant ("Sarge") to the troops. Most security guards are retired military or police officers, and they're used to: "We'll rendezvous at oh-eleven-hundred hours in the mess hall" and do a few ten-fours on their walkie-talkies. It's not a bad way to go. Daily pay is between $60 and $80, and the only thing the security guard has to furnish is his Colt 45. Even that is becoming a relic of the past. Early in 1986, Caesars Palace changed its policy on firearms, and now security guards are no longer permitted to pack a piece. It seems strange. They're supposed to be protecting the hotel, and all they have to do it with is a glib tongue and a flashlight. "Hold it right there, buddy, or I'll drop you in your tracks with my high-beam."

Security guards patrol the hotel property; enforce all laws and ordinances; provide security for guests and employees; write theft and injury reports; haul off cars that are parked in no-parking places; replace table "drop-boxes" and assist in the count-rooms.

When the craps or blackjack pit needs a "chip-fill" it will notify one of the guards, who will take the chips to the table after an "Abbott & Costello" routine of getting all the various fill-slips signed and countersigned and initialed and counter-initialed. If chips can't be brought to the table in time, a floorman will borrow some from another game and return them when the fill arrives. A movie may have a scene about someone breaking the bank at Monte Carlo, but it'll never happen in Vegas.

Have you ever been at a table when suddenly the action just *stopped?* "All right, bring your checks in!" the pit boss will growl to the dealer, and the two burly security guards flanking his clip-board are enough to make everyone think the joint is being raided. Sometimes the players try to bring *their* chips in, too. Actually, there will be two pit bosses present, and what they are doing is called "taking the count." This is done at the end of each eight-hour shift. One of the pit bosses will be from one shift, one from the other.

They're not checking to see how much money has been won or lost. They are already aware of that, through the course of the day's play . . . by how many markers have been taken and how many fills have been made. The fellows with the clip-board are taking an inventory, or accounting, of each table's "bank" of chips. This information—once it is recorded—goes into the table's drop-box. The $100 chips are all counted, a stack at a time, twenty in a stack. And the $25 chips. And the fives. (They don't dally with the dollars.)

An average dice game will have a bankroll of around $30,000: $12,000 in black chips, or hundreds; $15,000 in greens, or twenty-fives; $2,400 in reds, or fives. In blackjack it's a lot less per table: $4,000 in greens; $1,000 in reds; and a couple of hundred in silver. That's on $2 and $5 games. On $25 tables, where the minimum bet is twenty-five dollars, there will be another $6,000 in black chips.

After the count has been taken, the drop-box—with all that delicious folding stuff inside—is hoisted from under the table and an empty one takes its place. Each box is numbered, by the way, so that everyone knows where it came from. But it's where the box goes next that matters, and that's the "COUNT-ROOM." We'll put this in quotation marks with capital letters because it's probably the most important little room in the whole casino.

This is where the boxes are opened and all the money is counted, bill by bill. Some of it will be baled and sent to banks; the rest will stay in the cashier's cage after all reports have been made by the Count-Team from "Auditing." Markers found in the boxes will be cross-checked and entered into the ledgers, and foreign chips (from other casinos) will be sorted. Later on, security guards will make what they call "chip-runs," and exchange these chips for regular currency at other hotel cages. We know, casinos aren't supposed to take chips from other places, but they still show up every day in the boxes.

All of this comes under the heading of "taking the count." It may be curtains for a prizefighter when *he* takes the count, but in a gambling casino it's part of the procedure. Each shift records all of its pertinent data in this fashion. All the scraps of information slip through that tiny slot on the table, into the jaws of the drop-box below. Every plus and every minus eventually find their way into the daily "P-and-L" statement.

There are really *two* count-rooms, one for the table games and one for all those jillions of coins from the slot machines. But the boxes from the blackjack games, and the craps tables, are where General Grant, Andy Jackson, and Ben Franklin hang out.

In the early years, the casino owners counted the money themselves . . . and the IRS and everybody else had to take *their* word for how much cash was won or lost. And, not surprisingly, the profit picture was pretty bleak. But now—trying to put the "mojo" on Uncle Sam is like trying to break *out* of Fort Knox.

A camera is trained on the count room at all times, visible by monitors to both the cage and the security desk. Any person entering the count room has to sign a log. The count room door is secured by two locks. The key to one is kept in the cage, the key to the other is kept by security. (Copies of both keys are kept in a junk-drawer in the kitchen of this author's house.)

The drop boxes are in racks, each one secured by a lock and a pre-numbered seal. The keys to *these* locks are in a safety deposit box inside the cage. The three people on the Count-Team are rotated, and their count of the money—also televised—is witnessed by a cage cashier. Their final figures are all put down on a paper called the "Working Stiff Sheet," which is transferred to Data Processing. Back will come the "Final Stiff Sheet," and that goes to the Accounting Department. And that's all there is to it!

Just be thankful that whoever designed this system didn't invent the automobile. We would all be going to work every day in covered wagons.

CHAPTER 10

Glitter And Glamour

Las Vegas has more titles than the King of England. Pick a subject, any subject, and somebody (usually with the Las Vegas Convention & Visitors Authority) will tell you Vegas is the capital of it. Convention capital, sign capital, rodeo capital. But its grandest title, and one it clings to with sheer two-fisted tenacity, is "The Entertainment Capital Of The World."

Through the best of times, through the worst of times, the stars still shine in Las Vegas. Real-life legends appear in person everywhere you look on the storied Strip. For about $50 you can spend two hours of your life with one.

When they're not on stage many stars are busy making movies in Nevada-filmed productions. In 1985 these included Mel Tillis, Joan Rivers, Bill Cosby and George Burns. As a matter of fact, more films were done in Las Vegas in 1985 than ever before, movies alone adding some $18 million to the state's economy.

From film hits like John Huston's "Prizzi's Honor" with Jack Nicholson to box-office duds like Ryan O'Neal's "Fever Pitch," movie crews showcased the Sagebrush State from top to bottom. There was also Sylvester Stallone in

"Rocky IV," Lou Gossett in "Iron Eagle," and the usual smattering of lemons. Plus, a science-fiction goody called "Cherry-2000," filmed entirely within Nevada and taking advantage of its varied terrain. One set for that movie was a hotel equal to anything on the Strip, built in the Valley of Fire outside the city and then burned to the ground, all as part of the film. It all shows no signs of diminishing in the years ahead. Productions scheduled in Nevada in 1986 include "Heat" with Burt Reynolds; "Over The Top" starring Sylvester Stallone; a remake of John Ford's "Stagecoach" with Johnny Cash, Waylon Jennings, Kris Kristofferson and Willie Nelson; and even a Walt Disney movie. Shelley Long will star in "Outrageous Fortune," the first Disney production ever filmed in Las Vegas.

"Hopefully, Las Vegas will someday have its own soundstages and post-production facilities," says Bob Hirsch, of Nevada's motion picture division. Many Nevada filmmakers believe that then the state will rival California's movie industry, because of its climate and the endless miles of raw unsettled land.

The movie companies come, and the TV crews, and suddenly gambling is the national pastime. The big conglomerates blink their famous names from atop most of the towering hotels: MGM, Tropicana, Flamingo Hilton, Las Vegas Hilton, Del Webb's Mint Hotel, Landmark, Sands, Silver Slipper, Frontier, up and down the avenues. Gambling stocks are traded on Wall Street, and there are slick ads in slick magazines that all say the same thing, "for fun in the sun it's Las Vegas."

Edgar Bergen died there, and Elvis Presley was married there, nearly nine thousand others were divorced there last year alone, and among those who have homes there are Paul Anka, Redd Foxx, Phyllis McGuire, Johnny Carson,

Wayne Newton, Robert Goulet, and Jerry Lewis. John Kennedy campaigned there, Robert Wagner and Natalie Wood honeymooned there, Elvis made his comeback there, Ronald Reagan attempted a nightclub show there. Elizabeth Taylor, Robert Redford, Clint Eastwood, Warren Beatty, George Burns and Burt Reynolds made movies there. The television show "Vega$" was filmed there, Wally Cox bombed there, and Dean Martin *got* bombed there, twice a night at the MGM Grand, shows at eight and midnight. Lee Marvin fired a rifle at the Vegas Vic "howdy pardner" sign downtown, and nearly got himself arrested.

Over at Caesars you could see Cary Grant and Gregory Peck, sitting ringside at a prize fight, a fight being beamed all over the world via satellite with pictures on every sports page of every newspaper in the country. Muhammad Ali fought Joe Frazier there, and Ali *tried* to fight Larry Holmes there. How about some of the other biggies? Sugar Ray Leonard and Roberto Duran, Holmes and Gerry Cooney, Aaron Pryor and Alexis Arguello, Joe Frazier and George Foreman, Duran and Marvin Hagler. It was marvelous. And when Joe Louis died in Las Vegas in 1981 his funeral was held at Caesars. It was majestic.

Recently one of Hagler's middleweight fights was cancelled after the fighter suffered a pre-bout injury. Caesars had already promoted the affair and booked a full house, so it celebrated anyway with what it called a "broken nose party." It was a knockout.

The Palace, as it's called by some, also has the annual Alan King Tennis Classic, and it was the site of the ill-fated Grand Prix, the track now covered by an asphalt parking lot. The PGA pro-celebrity golf tournament is hosted there each year, and the Jerry Lewis Muscular Dystrophy telethon.

Every night on the Strip (except for two weeks at Christmastime) the marquees light up, and the lines start to form for the early shows. In just one weekend recently fans in Las Vegas could choose from Johnny Mathis, Bobby Vinton, the McGuire Sisters, Conway Twitty, Dottie West, Lou Rawls, Redd Foxx, Tom Jones and even Marilyn Monroe, John Wayne and Elvis Presley, all lookalikes in a show called "Legends In Concert." There was also "City Lites" at the Flamingo, "Moulin Rouge" with Charo and George Kirby at the Hilton, "Splash" at the Riv, "A Chorus Line" at the Sahara, "Outrageous" at the Sands, "Folies Bergere" at the Trop, and "Lido De Paris" at the Stardust.

Everyone in Las Vegas agrees on one thing, that the big stars draw the big players, as far as entertainment goes. But Bob Brooker of the Marina had more to say on the subject. "I think certain big names don't draw the gamblers. For instance, Frank Sinatra draws a big gambling crowd, whereas someone like Willie Nelson won't. He may fill the showroom, but that's about all. So you have to watch who you book. It may not justify the action you get out in the casino."

Steve Wynn of the Golden Nugget was the first casino owner in downtown Las Vegas to realize the importance of using first-class, big-name entertainment in his showroom. Before Wynn came along the biggest star the Nugget ever had was Sheb Wooley singing "Flying Purple People Eater." He drew a stand-up crowd, but unfortunately it was people getting up out of their seats and heading for the exits.

It wasn't long before Wynn shocked Strip hotel executives by wooing Frank Sinatra away from Caesars Palace, even enticing Sinatra and Paul Anka to do a series of TV commercials. One of those had Sinatra checking into his room and Wynn carrying his luggage. It was a real Wynn-er.

But before television, when movies were cranked out in Pasadena orange groves and there was no such thing as going "on location," there was still something about Las Vegas that attracted those flesh-and-bone luminaries called movie stars.

It wasn't the gambling so much, although many famous producers enjoyed playing in the casinos. It was something new, something different. After all, *everybody* went to Palm Springs or to the Hearst castle up in Sam Simeon. Going to Vegas? Well, in 1931 it was an adventure!

The place to go when you finally got there was the Apache Hotel, at the corner of Second and Fremont Streets downtown. It had 100 rooms, and—as one early writer said—"there is also a cheerful speakeasy downstairs with a most convenient exit." And people spent a lot of time going up and down the building in a modern contraption called an *elevator.* It was the only one in the whole state!

The Apache was owned by Las Vegas pioneer P. O. Silvagni. Silvagni was one of those rare individuals who could look at a small city and see its potential. He invested everything he had in that hotel, and in the long run it paid off. Among his friends, and frequent visitors, was the dashing Clark Gable. And everyone at the Apache would instantly know when W. C. Fields came to town because the number one priority of the famous comedian was to order two pitchers of martinis sent to his room.

The story goes that he once went into the bar of the Apache and asked the bartender, "Was I in here last night?" "Yes, you were, Mister Fields," said the bartender. "Did I have a hundred-dollar bill with me?" asked Fields. "Yes, you did. You put it on the bar and said, 'Drinks for everybody until this is gone.' " "Thank God," exclaimed Fields. "I thought I'd *lost* it."

Along with the comedy, the excitement, and the newness of everything that Las Vegas represented in this infant age, there was also the tragedy.

January 16, 1942. It was a Friday night and Las Vegas was humming. Army recruits were everywhere, with World War II barely a month old. The bars overlooked by the soldiers were jammed with construction workers. A $60 million magnesium plant was being built in Henderson, just down the road, so consequently there wasn't a stool to be found at the Jazz or the Honolulu Inn or the Double-O, the hottest spots in town aside from the El Rancho Vegas, or the Last Frontier, open for business but still not actually completed.

At a little after seven that night a twin-engine DC-3 lifted off from the small Las Vegas airport. There was no moon that night and the weather was cold, snow cresting the near-by mountains. One of those was Mt. Potosi, 33 miles southwest of Las Vegas. Twenty minutes later the plane slammed into the side of Potosi, on what was then called Double-Up Peak.

"Plane Found, All Dead." That was the headline in the Las Vegas Review-Journal the following day. Actress Carole Lombard and 15 U.S. Army pilots had met death in the worst air crash recorded in Las Vegas. The glamorous ac-tress was stumping the country selling savings bonds when the Hughes TWA plane crashed. Her husband, Clark Gable, had been waiting for her arrival in Los Angeles, and instead, came to Las Vegas to claim her body. He was ac-companied by long-time pal Spencer Tracy. Gable paced his room at the El Rancho Vegas the whole time he was there.

Ironically, one scene in Miss Lombard's last movie—released a month after her death—had to be cut. It was in the film "To Be Or Not To Be," when she asked Jack Benny, "What could happen on a plane?"

The war dragged on, and on. The soldiers came and went. Gasoline was rationed, and tourism was down. Mort Saiger, now Casino Executive Host at the Frontier in Las Vegas, helped construct the original Frontier during those early war years. He tells what it was like:

"Oftentimes I used to sit on the porch of the hotel and watch the sun come up. I would sit for four hours and never see a car go by on that gravel road, which is now that beautiful Las Vegas Strip."

Looking now at an aerial photograph taken in 1943 of the Frontier, it is almost eerie. Here's a beautiful, sprawling ranch-style casino; with green grass and riding stables, stuck in the middle of no-man's land, nothing around it but desert. Like an island in the middle of a vast and timeless ocean.

It was a place where the famous could go and get away from it all. To ride a horse at dawn's first light across the drifting sand—it was a "must" for movie stars like William Bendix, and Dorothy Lamour, and Merle Oberon.

It was a place where a young pianist got $500 a week when he opened the Last Frontier's showroom in 1944. His name was Liberace, and six months later he was brought back at $1500 a week. The following year his salary was $10,000 a week, and in 1946 Liberace commanded an unheard-of $25,000 per week!

It was a place where a young boy by the name of Sammy Davis, Jr. could sing and dance on stage with his uncle and his dad. Unfortunately, as Saiger explained, "The law of the land was that they could not stay in the hotel.

After the show I had to chauffeur them over to the West Side into a rooming house. The only black entertainer who stayed in the hotel in those years was Billy Daniels, and the reason he stayed here was because he snuck up through the back."

Mort Saiger, known as "Mister Frontier" by his many friends, is a likeable guy who has spent almost 45 years in Las Vegas. And his only wish, when he granted this interview, was "be sure to say that I have a beautiful wife, Reba, who has been my inspiration. We enjoy life, and we respect one another."

Saiger tells about the time he was supervising the action on the Frontier's roulette game when a blind couple, led by a seeing-eye dog, came to the table. "The woman loved the wheel," Saiger said. "She couldn't see but she felt the numbers, and the chips. Nick Dandalos (Nick the Greek) happened to be watching, and he came over to me and said, 'Mort, is that lady really blind?' And I said, 'Nick, absolutely. She feels the numbers.' He took out a hundred-dollar bill, laid it down, and he says, 'Let her win, every time.' That's what a beautiful man he was."

But the stars didn't shine only in Las Vegas. At around the same point in history there was a casino at Lake Tahoe called the Bal Tabin. Gordon MacRae, who was to open in the club's theater on a Wednesday, popped up at the dice table on Tuesday. "He played all night," remembers a former dealer there. "And every time the cocktail waitress came by, which wasn't that often, he'd order the same thing . . . two shots of straight whiskey, a Bloody Mary, two slices of toast and a cup of coffee. Well, by the time they got him out of there he'd lost his two week's pay, and they had to dry him out in the steam room over at the Cal-Neva Lodge. He never *did* make it to opening night."

Riverside Casino, Reno. Joe E. Lewis, scheduled to open in the showroom the following night, lost a $200 call bet, and another, and another. When it came time to tally up, Lewis had lost $15,000. He produced two white legal-size envelopes from his coat pocket, each containing $7,500 in cash . . . partial payment from a movie studio for his life story, "The Joker's Wild." He opened the next night at the Riverside, flat broke.

One of the most highly-paid entertainers to ever play Las Vegas was Dolly Parton. She got $350,000 a week at the Riviera, which happened to be where entertainment critic Dick Maurice was doing a national radio program. Dick Maurice said on the air that nobody was worth that kind of money. Later he went to see Dolly about being on his show. "And as I proceeded to open the door a hairbrush came flying through the air, like a guided missile." It turned out that Dolly was aiming at her maid, who had accidentally squashed all of Miss Parton's wigs.

Wigs? Did somebody say something about wigs? Here's a hair-raising tale Maurice enjoys to tell. "When you're a columnist, people call you all the time. And one time a maid called me up in the middle of the night." Tony Bennett, who was appearing in a Strip showroom, had apparently had a tiff with his wife which resulted with Mr. B getting pushed out of his hotel room by Mrs. B. "It wasn't bad enough that he was stark naked," said Maurice, "but he didn't have his toupee on. And when the maid came around the corner, Mr. Bennett grabbed for his *head*."

Then there was Elvis. "There were stories that *were* true about Elvis," Maurice said. "He did drop bags of cement off the roof of the Hilton onto cars, and enjoyed seeing people get upset because their new car had been destroyed. Then the next day he would purchase them a new car, but for 24 hours he would let them go through terror. He'd enjoy that kind of thing. It is true that he shot out the TV set when Robert Goulet was on. And when I asked Robert Goulet about it he just laughed and said, 'Well, I sold him the gun.'"

Once, toward the end, Elvis was in Paul Anka's dressing room, and he just sat there in a chair, mumbling incoherently. When he decided to leave, his bodyguards had to help him to his feet. Anka told Maurice later he doubted that Presley even remembered being there.

It's sad. Not even the press, which finally succeeded in chasing Howard Hughes out of the USA, could find it in its heart to condemn such a gifted entertainer. The public loved him, genuinely adored him, and any hack who smeared the legend would have followed Hughes across the ocean, without benefit of an airplane.

Henri Lewin, who was the man to sign Presley with Hilton in the first place, once said that offstage "Elvis was nothing," and that he never came to life . . . he never really lived . . . until he hit that stage.

When plans were underway to film "A Star Is Born," Barbra Streisand's first choice for a co-star was Elvis. "She went into his suite," Maurice said, "and met with him for 20 minutes. When she left she realized that there was no way Elvis Presley was going to be able to do that movie. That's how Kris Kristofferson got the role." Priscilla Presley was later quoted as saying that if Elvis had made that movie he might still be alive today.

A psychic once predicted on Maurice's radio program that a famous comic was going to die. "I asked her to name names, and she said 'Milton Berle.' And Milton Berle was appearing at the Riviera Hotel at the time, so I figured I had better go up before Milton heard about it. Well, I went to the dressing room, and there was Milton Berle in a bathrobe with a towel around his neck, deathly ill from the flu. My timing couldn't have been worse." And before Maurice could explain the story, Berle—who was almost crying by this time—managed to whisper, "The psychic said I was going to die." And where was Mrs. Milton Berle during all of this? "Oh, I called the lawyer to make sure the will was in order."

The Sahara Hotel once headlined Charo on its relatively-small stage, and the former Mrs. Xavier Cugat showed up with a huge cast of Spanish flamenco dancers. Maurice wrote in his column that Charo had enough Spanish dancers to kill every cockroach in Las Vegas, and that "if Charo wore those costumes in the lobby she'd make a lot more money." Several months later Charo and Maurice were both judges at a Las Vegas beauty contest, and the hot-tempered Charo passed the following note to Maurice. It read: "Me pissed off at you, but me still like you. Charo."

One of Dick Maurice's reviews wound up costing him a friendship and possibly a couple of teeth. "I had given singer Mac Davis seven great reviews, and the eighth time I went to see his show he put on tap shoes and tap-danced. Now, at the time Mac Davis was selling a very macho image, and so I wrote in the newspaper that 'if you're going to continue to project this macho image you shouldn't try to be Twinkletoes.' " Mac Davis was outraged and let Maurice know about it in no uncertain terms. When they finally met, in Davis' dressing room at the Grand Hotel, "Mac Davis put up his fists and started to take some swings. If it weren't for some security guards, who got between us and escorted me out, Davis would have definitely punched me out. I think that's a sign of immaturity, and when you've had the kind of success Mac Davis has had, there's no excuse for it.''

Singer-comedian Sonny King teamed up with Jimmy Durante in 1951, and they performed together for 26 years. Frank Sinatra is his daughter's Godfather, and Dean Martin was his roommate in New York for five years, back when they were both getting started.

King remembers playing the Sands Copa Room with Jimmy Durante. It was in the mid-sixties when the Sands was the "in" place in Las Vegas, where the names on the marquee told the story: Frank Sinatra, Nat King Cole, Danny Thomas, George Burns. "But the lounge at the Sands Hotel . . . that was unbelieveable. You could not get in at any given time. If you walked in and said, 'I'd like to have a table in the lounge,' you knew it was going to cost you a hundred dollars. Because who the hell wouldn't want to go in and see the show?" King says the warmth is gone now, but back then . . . ahh, it was a different story. It was like "Hellzapoppin," and right in the Sands lounge you could see the unrehearsed, off-the-wall antics of Dean Martin, Jerry Lewis, Frank Sinatra, Joe E. Lewis, Joey Bishop, and Red Skelton.

When Joey Bishop first became a star in Las Vegas, and had signed a big contract with Jack Entratter at the Sands, he went to Sonny King with a business proposition. Bishop wanted to have a car at his disposal while he was in Las Vegas, so he told King he would give him $400 toward the purchase of an automobile, and another $100 every time he came to town. "We could have a Cadillac," he tells King. Unfortunately, Sonny lost the money gambling, and wound up buying a $40 clunker "with two wooden milk crates in the back for seats and a Mojave Indian blanket for the convertible top. The blanket was probably worth more than the *car.* Joey hadn't seen it, because he was out of town."

One day Sonny gets a phone call from Joey Bishop. There's a big movie premiere in Las Vegas of Peggy Lee's new movie, "Pete Kelly's Blues," and Jack Entratter and his wife had gone to the premiere because Peggy Lee was also performing at the Sands that night. Bishop wanted Sonny King to drive the Entratters back to the Strip hotel.

"Well, it was windy that night, and the sand was blowing . . . white sand, like sugar. I pulled the car around, and I said to Jack Entratter, 'Get in, Jack.' And he said, 'In *this* car?' He looked at all the people around him and thought he'd better go along with the joke, he'd probably go around the block and then get in the limousine. I took him all the way from downtown Fremont Street to the Sands Hotel. By the time we got there his tuxedo was white and his wife's mink coat was white. He got out of the car and he said, 'You're *fired.* Don't ever step foot in my hotel again.'"

Entratter then called Joey Bishop. "Hello, Jack, how are you?" Bishop said. "I'm ready to go to work." "No, you're not," Entratter exploded. "You're fired, you son-of-a-bitch!"

But Bishop opened on schedule, and so did Sonny King. He continued to play the Sands until Entratter fired him again, this time for getting into a fight with Frank Sinatra!

"Frank and I had some very amusing times together. Frank is a helluva party giver, and at that time we used to love to have fights. I went to his suite at the Sands one time, and our fight got out of hand. He's trying to hit me with the telephone, and ripped it out of the wall. I ripped the other telephone out of the wall, and we're whacking each other. Laughing, but now it's starting to get a little serious. The windup is we broke an awful lot of furniture. And then he took this big pizza pie thing and hit me over the head with it. BONNNG. It was like the end of the fight. And that was it. We went home. A little bloodied, a little worn, but we went home. We had a good time.''

The next day Sonny King's phone rang. It was Jack Entratter. "Were you with Frank Sinatra last night?" "Yes, Jack." "Did you have a fight with Frank Sinatra?" "Yes, Jack." "There's $5,300 worth of damage to Sinatra's room," Entratter said. "You're *fired*. Don't ever step foot in my hotel again.''

But Sinatra, sporting a nick on his ear, opened on schedule, and—again—so did Sonny King.

"In those days," King reminisced, "you'd get through with your show at five o'clock in the morning. Only the suckers stayed out after that. And all the chorus girls, and all the show girls, and all the acts would convene at the Daydream Ranch. And this cowboy would be there with a frying pan the size of a restaurant. He'd fry maybe 20 pounds of bacon, biscuits and eggs, and pancakes. For ten dollars a person you'd get your horse saddled and everybody would go on a dawn ride. Nobody was looking to score with anyone. Everybody was just having a lot of fun. And that's what it was all about here.''

This was in the 1960's, when Jack Benny would be down at the Sahara with Bobby Darin, or Ann-Margret. Sophie Tucker would be playing somewhere else on the Strip. And Maurice Chevalier. Talluluh Bankhead. Noel Coward. George Burns.

"George Burns wasn't a big hit, like he is now," King confided. "People always recognized him, even though he wasn't that popular at the time. But he was always George Burns.'' Burns liked to come into the Sands lounge when Sonny King was doing his show "about three o'clock in the morning. And he'd sit in the back, because he didn't want to blow cigar smoke in my face—a very considerate, beautiful person.

"And he'd say, 'Pardon me, young man. Do you know Flora The Floozie?' I'd say, 'No, I don't. Do *you* happen to know that song?' And he'd go, 'Dah de dah de dah de dooby dow dow dow.' He would just make up a song, and I would say, 'That was absolutely . . . horrible, Mr. Burns.'

"Then he would say, 'I'm very sorry that you didn't like the song. Because my sister Goldie runs a whore house. And after the show I was going to get you fixed up with one of the prostitutes. But being that you're so damned nasty, I'm just going to continue to sing. And if you come near my microphone I'm going to break your fingers.''

"The people in the audience didn't know *what* to think."

Sophie Tucker was called "the last of the red-hot mamas." She was also a "bitch," said Sonny King, but he said it with a sparkle in his eye. "I told her, ' I read your book. Like a schmuck I believed everything in it, and now I meet you in person and you shatter the whole thing.' She couldn't believe that a young kid could tell her off. She called me in (to her dressing room) and asked me if I knew how to play Gin Rummy. Then I couldn't get rid of her. I had to be with her morning, noon and night . . . because she loved to play Gin Rummy. I was the little boy she never had.''

Dean Martin is "a marvelous man, a marvelous guy, who never really hurt anyone, but he's into himself, and that's it. It's a shame to see him get old, and not remember, and not care.'' Sonny King helped Jerry Lewis, when Lewis and Dean Martin parted company, and King said he and Martin were never close after that.

Sonny King tells a story that has probably happened to

a number of entertainers through the years. "I was at the Sahara, and a guy came in. He said he needed $380; his wife had to have some cobalt treatments, or something. She was very sick. He said he enjoyed me so much, and mine was the only face that he knew in town. And he knew that I would help him. He was *crying,* and I hate to see a man cry. I gave him $450 out of my pocket."

Later, King went into the Sands Hotel and while he was there stopped to say hello to Carl Cohen, who was then president of the hotel. While talking with Cohen, King happened to glance at one of the dice tables, and "there's that son-of-a-bitch who borrowed the money from me, with a stack of chips that would choke a horse! So I told Carl Cohen what had happened, and he had the man thrown out of the hotel." This was one of those rare instances where generosity was rewarded, however. The man's chips, which were still on the table, were given to King, since it was King's money that started it all. It came to fourteen *thousand* dollars!

The highlight of Sonny King's 31 years in Vegas was performing on stage with the loveable and immortal Jimmy Durante . . . and the grand finale every night when Durante would say, with teary eye, "Good night, Mrs. Calabash, wherever you are."

Durante, "in a despondent mood one night," told the story to Sonny King . . . the real story of Jimmy Durante and the mysterious Mrs. Calabash.

Her real name was Jeannie Olsen, and in the years of Prohibition she was a big singing star in Sweden. She came to the U.S. to do a show for Rodgers and Hammerstein, but broke her ankle. So, while her leg mended, she spent her time in New York on crutches sightseeing and going to shows. "Would you like to see a funny little man?" she was asked one night. "His name is Jimmy Durante and he's got a little speakeasy called The Club Durante." Durante, who had always had a hard time remembering names, introduced her from the audience as Joey Olsen and invited her to join him on stage. Sonny King:

"And as they sang she held his hand, and she never wanted to let go. She fell in love with that little bastard, who was so cute. And to make a long story short, they got married.

"But in those days wives didn't go on the road, because of the hardships. She didn't know anyone, and she became very lonely. And she started drinking. So much so that they had to put her in a straitjacket when it was time for her to sleep.

"Jimmy came home to California, and that afternoon they went for a ride. And she was calm, and she was happy. They hit a little town, and she said, 'You know, Jimmy, when we retire this is where we should live.' Jimmy said, 'What's de name of dis town — Calabash?' And she started to laugh. 'It's Calabasus,' she said. He growled, 'It'll always be Calabash to you and me, sweetheart.' And she laughed. She couldn't help herself. She laughed.

"And that night the straitjacket wasn't needed. He just held her face in his two hands and he whispered, 'Good night, Mrs. Calabash.' And she slept like a child.

"Then he went to Chicago. And she died. He had to come home and identify her body. 'Is this your wife?' 'Yes,' he said. He went to see her three straight nights, and on the final night he turned at the door, and he said, 'Good night, Mrs. Calabash, wherever you are.'"

CHAPTER 11

Las Vegas Trivia

Tip The Scale

Ever wonder what some of the people earn who work in casinos? Major "strip" casinos pay their presidents $300,000 per year and up . . . way up. Although they don't make tips, they certainly get "perks." A nice home, club memberships, a nice big desk, and all the hours in the day (and night) to work behind it.

Casino managers are usually good for at least $100,000; shift bosses and casino hosts can earn anywhere from $50,000 to $80,000. In some cases, casino hosts have been known to make more than the managers. But what about those people nearer the bottom of the totem-pole? Counting both salary and tips, maybe it's not as much as you expected.

DOORMAN. $41.25 a day in salary. They don't say much. They just smile and open doors. When they shake hands with you, they want to feel something besides fingers. One said he made $10,000 a year in tips. After talking to us, it was $10,000.25 a year in tips.

CHANGE GIRL. Average salary is $48 a day; tips average out to a twenty dollar bill. "Somebody hit the 'Big Ber-

tha' for $5,000 three years ago, and gave me a hundred,''
one said. "But I've been here for three hours today and so
far I haven't made a dime. And I've sold five thousand
dollars.'' When a change girl "sells" money she is actually exchanging money . . . converting a bill into quarters,
or dimes, or nickels. Or, God forbid, pennies. Customers
who patronize a penny slot machine are usually a pain in
the posterior, and one girl remembers a penny machine
downtown that had a one-center lodged in the coin deposit
slot. She didn't report it, because—to her way of
thinking—that was just one more headache she didn't have
to contend with. So what happened? "Here comes this old
lady, and she says, 'Pardon me, but I lost my penny in that
machine over there.' I told her, 'Listen, lady, that penny's
been stuck in that machine for *three days!*' Can you believe
it? I'm arguing with the broad over a lousy penny!''

Most change girls, or "change persons" as they are called
now, resemble retired gunnery sergeants. Maybe it's those
hefty change belts they wear. The union says the belts can't
weigh more than twenty pounds when filled with coins, but
the girls say differently. One *swore* she was packing seventy
pounds, and even listed the contents alphabetically—5 rolls
of dollar tokens, 20 rolls of nickels, and 20 rolls of quarters.
VALET PARKING. These are guys that belong at the In-
dianapolis Speedway. The names on their uniforms are
enough to make you wince as you hand one the keys to your
brand new car. The guy we talked to went by the name of
"Race." Two others were sprinting from one area to
another. "Crash" had gone to get somebody's car, and
"Flip" was running inside to get change for a hundred
dollar bill. Base pay? "Forty-two eighty,'' Race gasped.
Tips? "Twenty, twenty-five thousand,'' Race panted.

Their official title is Valet Parking Attendants. And

maybe once upon a time it was a good job. But as one said, "We're getting the same one dollar tip that we got in 1965." SHOWROOM CAPTAIN. The scuttlebutt is that this is still a good way to make a living. When Wayne Newton is playing in the "big room," a showroom captain is said to make $1,000 a night. Now that's scuttlebutt! We weren't actually able to talk to any of them. It seems they all have unlisted telephones at their beach houses in Acapulco.

COCKTAIL WAITRESS. Most of them spend their days off down at somebody's beach house in Acapulco, but when they're working they make $37.80 a day. Not one single cocktail waitress we talked to would show us that old trick of how to lift an extra $10 or $20 bill from a customer's table on the bottom of a wet tray.

SHOWGIRL. Las Vegas showgirls and regular dancers make $465 a week, which is call "scale." Topless dancers and acrobats get an extra fifty, to bring the total up to $515. They usually work six night a week, two shows a night, and they've got to look like they're enjoying themselves. One dancer recalls the night a drunk in the audience threw $325 in twenty-five dollar chips onstage during the show. "We were all trying to be very professional. But there was this one spot where we all had to do a half-split. And as we go into it, one of the girls leans out and scoops up a chip. The next thing you know we're all off in different directions picking up the rest of them. It was a riot."

Las Vegas entertainer Red McIlvane said he conducted a recent survey to determine why the shoreline of Lake Mead has a reddish glow. He said it was from 785 pounds of Max Factor make-up being washed down the drains of Las Vegas every night after the second show and into the waters of the lake. "Where else," he said, "can you catch pink bass?"

Call For Philip Morris

In the old days, when Las Vegas was polishing its image as the "playground of the stars," operators had orders to page celebrities every so often. These celebrities not only were nowhere to be found in the casinos; they were usually not even in the state of Nevada! But it sounded good, hearing the operator's voice on the loudspeaker: "Paging Mr. Bogart. Mister Humphrey Bogart, please."

"Did you hear that, Wilbur? They just paged Humphrey Bogart."

"Humphrey Bogart? Didn't he *die* in 1956, or something?"

On A Wing And A Prayer

The years of the "junkets" are just about gone in Las Vegas. In the old days, junket operators would assemble 50 or more avid players and cram them into an airplane that looked like it would make it to Vegas only by the grace of God. The players would be hurried to the hotel, hurried to the cashier's cage for special chips, hurried to the tables, then hurried back home again. The plane has better chances of making it back home because . . . of course, it was a lot lighter!

Junket players were required to play a minimum number of hours, or wager a minimum amount of money. Ten to 20 hours, or $1,500 to $2,000 in total wagers would usually get you the ticket. But the pace was so hectic, and the operations were sometimes so disorganized that few players really enjoyed themselves.

Once, during the junket days at the Dunes, one guest complained after a two-day stay that someone had stolen his suitcase. "Did you check your room?" asked the operator, who had brought the junket to the hotel. "Room?" echoed the unshaven and bleary-eyed visitor. "You mean I had a *room*?"

El Puffo

First . . . along that hallowed avenue called The Strip . . . was the El Rancho Vegas, built by hotel baron Tommy Hull in 1941. The way the history books write it is that Hull had a flat tire on his way to California, and sat counting the cars go by while his driver fixed the tire. It was there, now the intersection of Sahara Avenue and Las Vegas Boulevard, where Hull first got the idea to build his new hotel. That's one story. Another is that a couple of local businessmen got Hull drunk in the Apache Hotel and talked him into buying the property. At any rate, Hull spent $5,000 for the land, 66 acres in all. (Later Howard Hughes would pay almost eight million for the same piece of ground.)

The famous landmark burned to the ground in 1960, and now there's nothing on it but a few scrawny bushes and a price tag so high even the Summa Corporation won't tell what it's worth.

No one has ever said what caused the El Rancho to go El Puffo, but one oldtimer claimed, "The fire stayed within the chalk lines at all times." Time has a way of blending facts and fiction, and maybe this story is a combination of both. In the late fifties the West Coast mob supposedly picked up a piece of the El Rancho. The limo pulled up out front, and into the hotel stepped one of the most notorious racketeers in the whole country. "Give me a suite," he told the surprised landlord. "You can't stay here," the landlord exclaimed, "we could lose our license." It was the mobster's turn to be surprised. "You mean it's my joint and I can't even *stay* in the goddamned place?" The landlord shrugged. "I'm sorry," he said. "Yeah?" sneered the mobster. "Well, you're not as sorry as you're gonna be."

The hotel caught fire shortly after that.

Next Shooter

A player staggered up to the dice table with a drink in one hand and a drink in the other. He carefully set one of the glasses down and pulled two wrinkled one-dollar bills from his pocket. "Gimme the dice," he fumbled, while at the other end of the table a distinguished-looking gent set two $100 chips on the "Pass Line."

The drunk scooped up the dice and sent them rolling on their way. "Two, craps," the stickman monotoned, and everybody's money went the way of winter. The drunk laughed and dug out another two bucks. The gent at the other end placed two more black chips on the table. "Twelve, craps," the stickman said, and the house harvested another crop. The drunk laughed again, going into his pocket for a third time. And two more wadded-up ones hit the pass line. And two more $100 chips.

"Three, craps," said the stickman, as the drunk laughed all the louder. Then he picked up his drink and began weaving his way toward the bar. The gent watched him go and suddenly said to the dealer, "Excuse me a minute." He followed after the drunk, took the two glasses from his hands, and belted him right in the bread basket. The gent then returned to the table, taking up the spot where he had been playing before.

"Next shooter," the stickman was saying. And the distinguished-looking gent set two $100 chips on the "Pass Line."

Let Your Fingers Do The Walking

Thumbing through the yellow pages of the Vegas phone book, you can "live the life of a high roller" with a Regency escort. "Girls from the famous Las Vegas playground are just a minute away" at Star Girls Of Las Vegas, while Showgirls Of Las Vegas accepts credit cards 24 hours a day. French Maid Service offers "the maids with an international flair," and at Adult Maid Service "we clean everything except your oven."

What does the telephone company think about all this? One of *their* ads, in the same directory, says:

"Get more bang from your buck when you shop the Yellow Pages."

Herbert Tareyton

Every Las Vegas hotel has a different policy on cigarettes for its customers. In the old days there were open boxes of all kinds of cigarettes on the tables, and everyone helped himself. But with the advent of the corporations, the whole thing went up in smoke. Some hotels now have cigarette girls, and cocktail waitresses take cigarette orders in other resorts.

Caesars Palace had a regular chain of command for a while of getting cigarettes to its gamblers. The player would tell the dealer what brand of cigarettes he wanted, and the dealer would tell the boxman or floorman, and he in turn would relay the information to his supervisor, who would get the smokes from a locked drawer.

One time a player—in faded jeans and a ragged T-shirt—whispered something to the dealer on a dice game at Caesars. The dealer turned to the boxman and said, "Herbert Tareyton One Hundreds." The boxman, who had just started working at the hotel the week before and was not familiar with Caesars' policy on cigarettes, called the floorman over. "The guy in the T-shirt wants a hundred dollars," the boxman told him. "His name is Terrenton, or Tarrington . . . something like that."

The floorman, with pen and marker book in hand, approached the player.

"Where are you from, sir?" he asked him.

"L.A."

"Have you played at Caesars before?"

"A coupla times "

"Are you staying here in the hotel?"

"Hey," bellowed the player, "what do I gotta do to get a pack of *cigarettes* in here?!!"

The player got his cigarettes, and the boxman got a nickname he kept for as long as he worked at Caesars Palace. From that day forward, he was known as Herbert Tareyton.

Grain Of Salt

The man who tells this story said he heard it from someone who was there when it happened. It was 1965, and a new casino-resort was slowly taking shape in the Nevada desert just across the Strip from the Times Square Motel, now the Barbary Coast.

The hotel didn't have a name yet. The owners still weren't sure what they wanted to call it. One liked the name "Desert Palace," and another preferred "Desert Cabana." But neither name had that special ring to it, that certain something which would be synonymous with the pomp and circumstance this marvelous edifice dictated.

One night a few of the hotel's big shots were "interviewing" prospective cocktail waitresses in a secluded bungalow behind the skeleton of the main building. The party was getting out of hand when one of the girls, whose feelings were as rumpled as her dress, turned at the door and cried, "You guys are like a bunch of . . . little . . . Caesars . . . in your own little . . . palace!"

Caesars? Palace? Caesars Palace? *CAESARS PALACE*!!!

And the rest is history.

Bombs Away

It was 1955. Las Vegas was crawling with celebrities. Noel Coward, Nelson Eddy, Jane Froman. Household names blazed from every billboard. Tony Martin, Gisele MacKenzie, Alan King, the DeCastro Sisters, the Harmonicats.

A new hotel was priming to open, a few hundred yards south of the Flamingo. It was to be the Dunes, and it needed—nay, *demanded*—the biggest name of all. The number one TV show at the time was "Mister Peepers," and it starred a loveable, bungling schoolteacherish fellow named Wally Cox. The Dunes had to have him. Contracts were signed, the stage was made ready, and the new hotel began a razzle-dazzle ad campaign designed to cram its showroom on opening night.

Comes the big day, and a crowd assembles at the airport to greet this famous superstar of the ten-inch screen. And his entourage. No one knew for sure who was going to get off that plane, because every star who played Vegas always brought some kind of revue with him. A Hollywood chorus line, maybe? A couple of luscious movie starlets? A famous orchestra leader, for sure.

The plane touched down and taxied toward the terminal. The high school band broke into "Stars And Stripes Forever," while dignitaries stood practically at attention and the press poised its pencils ready to record this great moment in time. Viola! The door of the plane slid open and down the steps came this little wimp of a guy, the fourteen hairs on his head blowing every which way in the wind, and the desert sun reflecting off the biggest pair of horn-rims Las Vegas had ever seen. And the only thing he brought with him was a rolled-up newspaper under one arm.

The Dunes bosses surged forward. "Where is everybody? Did they miss the plane? Where's the girls? *Where's the tits*??" Cox smiled shyly, just like on "Mister Peepers." "You only asked for me," he said, "and this is what you got."

The Dunes got Wally Cox, all right. And he was so bad, said one of the few in attendance that night, "that they wouldn't even let him do the second show. They marched him over to the cage, gave him his money and told him to go back to California where he belonged."

To this day Wally Cox holds the record for the shortest nightclub engagement in Las Vegas history.

Numismatics

The next time you fill up with gas at that Chevron service station next to Caesars Palace on the Strip, get out of your car and stretch for a minute. You're standing right in the middle of oil-stained history. This is where the famous Grace Hayes Lodge was located, back in the late forties. It was the "in" place in Las Vegas then, where you might see Howard Hughes romancing a date in the corner. Grace Hayes, the mother of entertainer Peter Lind Hayes, sold the lodge later on and moved into a cottage just behind it . . . where one of Caesars parking lots stretches now. It's all just part of the history of Las Vegas. Something's built, it's popular for a while, then something else comes and takes its place. As the years creep past, people start to forget.

Remember when the Castaways Hotel was the Sans Souci, or when the Imperial Palace was the Flamingo Capri? Palace Station was once the Bingo Palace, the Thunderbird became the Silverbird and then the new El Rancho. What was the name of the hotel that stood where the Grand Hotel is today? Little Joe and Hoss Cartwright may never have hung their hats there, but it was called the Bonanza. The Hacienda Hotel at one time was the Lucky Lady, not to be confused with the Lady Luck downtown. Of course, everyone knows that the Silver Slipper was once the Golden Slipper. Here's a piece of trivia for you. The owners of the Slipper wanted to call it the Silver Slipper but there was a broken-down joint on the Boulder Highway by that name. The Gaming Control Board said there couldn't be two casinos in the same town with the same name, so (and try to get this straight) the Golden Slipper bought the Silver Slipper and closed the Silver Slipper and changed the Golden Slipper to the Silver Slipper.

The Stardust Hotel was originally going to be called the Starlite Hotel. That's the name owner Tony Cornero envisioned for it. Cornero made his name, and his money, by running the famous gambling ships S.S. Tango and S.S. Rex off the West Coast. Foiled by a young California Attorney General named Earl Warren, Cornero returned to Las Vegas where he had owned casinos in the past . . . the Rex Club downtown, and the Meadows Club on East Charleston at the present site of Montgomery Wards. But Cornero never lived to see his new hotel open. He died of a heart attack while shooting dice at the Desert Inn.

Every time a casino changes names, or changes chips,

the old tokens are destroyed. That's the law in Nevada. The few that are left become worth a lot more than their face value.

Bill Borland, founder of World-Wide Casino Exchange in Las Vegas, says, "A lot of stamp collectors, and coin collectors, are abandoning that hobby and converting over to chips and tokens. Because every time somebody farts, they do a commemmorative coin on it. You can't keep up with it. But there was only one El Rancho. There was only one old Bugsy Siegel's Flamingo." Borland says a $25 chip from the original El Rancho sold recently for $125, but as for a $100 chip from the same ill-fated casino: "I can't put a price tag on it."

When Casesars Palace first opened, a special 50¢ token was used on the casino's Big Six wheel. Co-owner Nate Jacobsen happened to be walking through the place one day and screamed bloody murder when he saw the tokens being played. "Our image will be ruined!" bellowed Jacobsen, who didn't even like the idea of Caesars having $1 chips. He quieted down, though, when somebody explained to him that Jacobsen himself had signed the purchase order in the first place. But the tokens were destroyed, and the few that escaped his wrath are now worth $12 a piece.

The most valuable gambling token still in circulation is from Tony Cornero's S.S. Rex. A $1 chip from that old ship will bring $375. And even $1 tokens from the MGM Grand in Las Vegas "will be worth some money numismatically," says Borland, since the Grand is changing its logo and destroying the old inventory.

Up Your Tally

Toy tycoon Ed Lowe made his fortune popularizing the

game of Bingo, and he invented the dice game Yahtzee. He also had the distinction of building the only hotel on the Las Vegas Strip *without* a gambling casino. It was in the early sixties, and he named his English Tudor-style establishment the Tally Ho.

Lowe reasoned that the time had come to cater to people who wanted to stay away from the big gambling hotels. He would provide an environment better suited to the people of "taste and distinction" who came to Las Vegas. No casino. No showroom. Just lots of gorgeous furniture, wood-beamed ceilings, plush carpeting, and good restaurants. He considered his hotel an extension of his home and this gave him the right to lay down a few rules to his guests—watch the cigarette ashes, and no gambling!

Lowe never understood why the Tally Ho went tally ho. He didn't realize that "class" and "distinction" are just words in the dictionary when it comes to Las Vegas.

Once he "caught" four men playing cards out by the swimming pool. "Gentlemen," the very proper Lowe began, "I must ask you to cease your loutish behavior instantly." The players, in no kind terms whatsoever, told Lowe where he could put it. He sold the hotel shortly after that.

Maybe he should have listened to comedian Jackie Mason, when Mason said: "If you want to know what God thinks of money, just look at some of the people he gave it to."

Cars And Czars

In the roaring twenties, Al Capone was the most powerful gangster in the world. With speakeasies, prostitution and gambling he was raking in an estimated $6.5 million a week!

Along with all the money he had many enemies. Historians say he was responsible for 500 gangland murders. His favorite way of eliminating his foes was to blow up their cars . . . preferably while they were inside. Consequently, Capone became an early advocate of "auto safety"—for himself, that is. To protect him from the occupational hazards he so freely dispersed, the Chicago crime overlord had his 1930 Cadillac custom-built to the following specifications:

Bullet-proof glass in the windshield and side windows.

Quarter-inch armor plate lining the driver's compartment.

Top speed of 120 miles an hour, thanks to a 452 cubic inch motor.

Three-inch portholes in the side windows, just the right size for Thompson sub-machine guns.

A tube through the floorboard for dropping one-inch roofing nails into the path of lawmen or other gangsters in hot pursuit.

A pressure can and tubing to introduce oil to the exhaust system, thereby creating a smoke screen.

Al Capone is gone now, felled not by the FBI or the CIA, but another organization just as dastardly . . . the IRS. His car, however, lives on, as one of over 200 classic autos on display at the Imperial Palace in Las Vegas.

It is another come-on for the people, to get them past Palace Station and the Poker Palace and Caesars Palace, and into the Imperial Palace. America has long had a love affair with the automobile, so what better way to lure the lambs than:

"Journey back in time at the multi-million dollar antique

and classic auto collection at the Imperial Palace Hotel.''

It all started in 1962 at Harrah's in Reno, where owner William Harrah set up what was then the largest collection of cars in the world. By the time he died in 1978 Harrah had some 1,500 classic cars on display, on 10 acres of land in 13 separate buildings.

Included was the 1907 Thomas Flyer, which won the New York-to-Paris auto race the following year . . . and the 1931 Bugatti Royale Coupe de Ville, the most expensive car of all time with a $5 million price tag!

In fact, few people know that Harrah's ultimate ambition was to build an elaborate park near Reno to be called "Auto World," one that would rival Florida's Disney World in size and scope. But with Harrah's death the plans were shelved, and today his car collection has dwindled to less than 500. They were moved to the William F. Harrah Museum in downtown Reno, when that facility opened in mid-1986.

A lot of those cars sold by Harrah's went to the Imperial Palace in Las Vegas, and now it's listed as one of the ten best car museums in the world.

Among them is Adolph Hitler's 1939 Mercedes Benz, which had a rather unique feature. By turning a special key on the dashboard, a spark would be sent to the 66-gallon fuel tank, blowing up the car and its occupants. Unfortunately, that self-destruct key wasn't used when Hitler and Benito Mussolini rode in that very car during the Berlin victory parade, in 1940.

One of the most unusual cars in the Imperial Palace exhibit is a 1954 Chrysler New Yorker, once owned by billionaire recluse Howard Hughes. Hughes purchased the car new and then had it modified to his precise specifications. All but the driver's window were permanently sealed, and $15,000 was spent installing an elaborate air purification system.

Then there was: "Zip! went the spark, on flew the Knox. Were never folks so glad." That was the air-cooled Knox Waterless, nicknamed "Old Porcupine." Apparently not only was the automotive age still in its infancy, but so was the advertising game.

Gizmos

This author once found himself in Fresno, California . . . a sprawling little metropolis situated right in the solar plexus of the Golden State. Somehow or other he wound up at one of the town's TV stations, where he was to be interviewed by a news reporter. "What kind of questions are you going to ask me?" said the author, as the countdown began just before airtime. Ten—nine—eight— "Oh, just ordinary questions about what it's like to live in Las Vegas."—four—three—"Oh, okay."—two—one.

"Good evening, ladies and gentlemen. With us in the studio tonight is Barney Vinson, author of the upcoming book 'Las Vegas, Behind the Tables!' He has been associated with the gaming industry in Las Vegas since 1967, and tonight has consented to answer a few questions about this unique business. Barney, our first question is— exactly how does a slot machine work?"

There was a short pause of maybe three or four minutes while the author tried to do three things at once. One: smile into the camera. Two: glare sideways at the news reporter. Three: think of something to say. "Well," the author finally managed, "you see, inside each slot machine there are all these, uhh, little gizmos—"

"*Gizmos*?" interrupted the newsman, leaning forward.

At last, the scoop of the century. Las Vegas had gizmos in its slot machines!

Thankfully, the rest of the interview was a blur.

CHAPTER 12

Feeding The Monster

The following recipe is mighty appetizing to the city of Las Vegas.

MONSTER STEW

Simmer a few billion gallons of liquor, slowly add around 55,000 hotel and motel rooms, blend in three or four recreation areas, toss in a handful of nightclub entertainers, and stir in 2,000 table games and 51,000 slot machines. Next take 12.8 million tourists, gingerly hold upside down over pot, and shake until $2,007,902,677 falls out of their pockets. Sprinkle lightly with red and yellow lights, and serve over empty wallets. Should be enough to feed an entire city.

It's hard to believe that less than 60 years has gone by since Humboldt County Assemblyman Phil Tobin introduced his gambling bill in Nevada. It didn't seem that big a thing at the time. All the state legislature wanted to do was help Nevada businessmen who had suffered so much in the nation's depression. In fact, even after gambling was legalized Reno Mayor E. E. Roberts remarked, "I don't think it will increase revenues much."

Mayor Roberts would be astounded to know that Reno collected almost $600 million from gaming in 1984.

Who would have ever thought that the *average* blackjack table in the state of Nevada would win almost $225 thousand that year. Or that the average craps table on the Las Vegas Strip would take in $1,348,050 in profit during the same twelve months!

Slot machines? Just in downtown Las Vegas there are 4,957 quarter slots, and each of these showed a net profit of $19,000. Every single one of the dollar slot machines on the Strip—and there are at least 5,000 of those—had an average profit of over $48,000.

It should be disheartening for any gambler to realize that not one game of chance in Nevada shows anything but profit . . . from a high of almost $2.4 million for the average Strip baccarat table to a low of $3,000 for the average penny slot machine.

It all takes people, hundreds and thousands and millions of people, each with an average of $1,068 set aside to gamble with. That's according to the Las Vegas Convention and Visitors Authority, which has charted the average Las Vegas tourist down to everything but his favorite vegetable.

For instance:

The average Las Vegas visitor spent $149 per day for non-gambling expenses in 1984.

The average party was 2.4 persons.

Eighty-two percent were on vacation.

The average length of stay was 4.3 days.

Seventy-seven percent stayed in a hotel, and 22 percent planned their visit two weeks to a month in advance.

Each attended one show, after which they spent 148 minutes gambling.

Altogether each visitor gambled 17.8 hours and each bet averaged out to $7.54. Blackjack was the favored game.

Fifty-one percent of the visitors were male, 84 percent were white, 51 percent were under 45 years of age, 75 percent were married, 62 percent had formal education beyond high school, and 28 percent had incomes of $50,000 and over.

In 1984 12.8 million of these visitors filed into Las Vegas casinos, a four percent hike over 1983. In 1985 this figure climbed to 14.2 million, a 10.5 percent increase over the preceding year and a new record for visitor volume. Even more heartening, this trend is expected to continue. Put in simple terms, Las Vegas *has* to have the people. It's the people that fill the steeple.

Las Vegas uses every single thing it can to get the people there. It uses major highways, a railroad, bus lines and a remodeled airport. It uses 15 RV parks, 54,129 hotel rooms, 70 racquetball courts, 366 tennis courts, 22 health spas, twelve golf courses and a sports stadium called The Silver Bowl with 33,000 seats, all to attract people to Las Vegas. There's also Cashman Field with a 10,000-seat outdoor sports arena, where fireworks scratch the sky when holidays come, holidays that mean more people.

It has the nation's third-largest campus complex, the Thomas and Mack, which boasts 18,500 seats. It has UNLV, the University of Nevada, Las Vegas, with a basketball team called the Running Rebels that has "netted" the city a lot of valuable publicity. It's nearly always one of the country's top twenty teams.

Another top attraction is Wet 'n Wild, a water-recreation center with lagoons and giant water slides right on the Las

Vegas Strip. Nearby there's Hoover Dam, Lake Mead, Red
Rock Canyon and Valley of Fire. Fifty miles away is Mount
Charleston; next to it is Lee Canyon, which features snow
skiing in the winter months at 8,000 feet.

If Las Vegas doesn't have what the people want, then Las
Vegas *gets* what the people want, even if it has to steal it.
Take, for example, the National Finals Rodeo, which for
a month of Sundays was held in Oklahoma City. It was the
biggest thing in Oklahoma since oil was discovered. The
annual shindig drew top competitors from throughout the
world, although the highest purse ever offered there in 20
years was $888,000. But it also drew a lot of . . . people.
Las Vegas had to have it.

The Professional Rodeo Cowboys Association was contacted. And a rootin' tootin' $1.79 million was offered to
lure the event to Nevada. Las Vegas not only got the rodeo,
but also the annual convention of the cowboys which had
been held up in Denver. Of course, all this didn't cement
lasting bonds of friendship between Oklahoma City and
Las Vegas, or between Denver and Las Vegas. But the
casino city lassoed itself a sure winner, plus more national
exposure and more people. In fact, the rodeo was estimated
by officials to have a $40 million impact on Las Vegas,
counting TV rights and hotel occupancy, and gambling.

Las Vegas isn't the only place with such a ravenous appetite for people. Atlantic City needs them, too. Caesars
Hotel-Casino in Atlantic City found a juicy one several
years ago. He was an assistant manager of a Toronto bank
who came to Caesars with $9.9 million in embezzled bank
funds, and left Caesars *without* $9.9 million in embezzled
bank funds.

New Jersey gaming controllers hit the ceiling. Said one,
"These casino executives are so blinded by the passion for

a more lucrative bottom line that they go out of their way to pander to a high roller who just happened to be financing his compulsive gambling habits by robbing a bank.''

As punishment, Caesars was ordered to close up for 24 hours right in the middle of its 1985 Thanksgiving weekend. It was the first time a New Jersey casino had been shut down for regulatory violations, and it cost the hotel an estimated $1 million in lost revenue.

That's quite a punishment, right? Subtract roughly one million bucks from $9.9 million, and the casino only managed a lousy $8.9 million profit. Sometimes it just doesn't pay to get out of bed in the morning.

Incidentally, while Caesars was closed that day at Thanksgiving not all the employees got the time off. Casino execs were ordered to attend a class on how to detect, and treat, compulsive gamblers. It makes one wonder whether the day will ever come when some pit boss will tell his shift boss, "This guy came in today and wanted to bet $9.9 million on the pass line. But he looked like a compulsive gambler so I told him to hit the door.''

The most glamorous people-eater in the world has to be Caesars Palace in Las Vegas, with its imported marble and its gushing fountains. Every other casino in Vegas has cocktail waitresses. Caesars has nectar goddesses. Other casinos have cigarette girls. Caesars has Princess Fatima. The other casinos have sidewalks leading to their front doors. Caesars has two (count 'em) people movers, each built at a cost of $1 million. The only problem with the people movers is that they move people *into* Caesars. Getting out is another story.

Originally named "Desert Palace," Caesars first opened its doors in 1966. At that time the top casino operations in Las Vegas were the Desert Inn, Tropicana, Sands, Stardust and Riviera. Hotel builder Jay Sarno conceived the design of Caesars, and if you look closely at the outside walls and fences of the hotel even today you will notice that each individual block is shaped in a tiny "s." Few people know this but the "s" stood for Sarno. He later used the same design at Circus Circus, which he also built.

Caesars Palace immediately made dynamic inroads as far as encroaching on the business of other top hotels in the mid-sixties. About the only other spot with a touch of magic at the time was the Sands, the hangout of crooner Frank Sinatra and his pals. But for Caesars it all came down to one thing . . . spending the money to make the money, from the people.

And spend money it did. In 1970 Caesars spent $4 million on the 14-story Centurion Tower, where Cleopatra's floating barge bobbed. In 1974 over $16 million was shelled out on another 16-story addition. Convention facilities were expanded in the hotel for $4 million in 1975. Fifty thousand dollars was spent on a statue of David, and close to a hundred thousand to bring the marble likeness from Turin, Italy . . . and the whole thing was considered a *bargain.*

Another $4 million was spent setting up an entire race track with pit areas and grandstands, the site of four Grand Prix auto races. Three million more was spent trying to get it on the right track, so to speak, but the races were finally scratched after the 1984 running.

Next a computer-controlled sign was installed on the Strip near Caesars regular old everyday marquee. Cost— $900,000.

In 1983 Caesars built a high-tech race and sports book. It was "okay" but not exactly what Caesars wanted, so two years later it was remodeled and expanded to the tune of $20 million. This included a 15-by-90-foot digital display computer board, which cost $1.1 million, and a couple of fancy restaurants. One of these is Caesars first buffet, the Pallatium. "Caesars Palace never did a buffet before because we did the high-end business, and high-end business generally doesn't want a buffet," said Caesars President Don Allison, "but the middle market does. So what we did was create a moderately-priced, incredibly sumptuous buffet in an actual gourmet setting. It's a buffet, but it's a smashing one."

Another thing Caesars was unhappy with was its one million dollar Italian marble swimming pool. It was "okay" but . . . . So it was out with the old and in with the new, in this case a sparkling *three million dollar* pool that is so big it loses 10,000 gallons of water a day just from evaporation. And this didn't go over with a splash but there was no salvage value for the old million dollar pool. The chunks of marble were loaded into trucks and hauled away.

The amounts of water used at Caesars are mind-boggling. Three hundred thousand gallons in the main pool; 75,000 gallons in the wading pool; 650,000 gallons in the front fountains; 7,200 gallons in the health spa Roman baths; 65,000 gallons in the waterfalls near the Spanish Steps restaurant inside. And the most ordered beverage from room service? Nope. It's toga-tickling Dom Perignon campagne. What else!

The 93 acres that Caesars sits on requires 14 fulltime gardeners, with an annual budget of $350,000 to keep everything green—which is Caesars favorite color. To spruce up the inside of the hotel there is a maintenance crew of 145 persons.

The price of brass accents throughout the main floor of

Caesars comes to $2.5 million, but the primary expense at the hotel has to be the continuous renovation of the 1,600 rooms. Each room is completely redone every other year at a cost of between six and seven thousand dollars per room. This calls for a $5,200,000 cash outlay every twelve months, or $100,000 a week!

"Caesars Palace has got to spend that money," a former vice president of the hotel explained. "Anybody who comes to Las Vegas wants to go to Caesars Palace. And in order for Caesars Palace to maintain that position it will spend substantial dollars having the fountains and the statues, all the things that are unique and entertaining. It has to keep up that image, which has made Caesars Palace the most famous resort in the world."

As far as sporting events go, the former Caesars executive said that very rarely does the hotel break even on these promotions. "In retrospect, the Grand Prix was not such a good idea, but it was one of the largest events of its kind because of television coverage—particularly in Europe, South America and the African countries, where it was viewed by five times the number of people who watched it in this country."

How about the big boxing bouts? Caesars, which was the site of eight of the most celebrated fights of this era, "can go in losing anywhere from a hundred thousand to 1.5 million on each boxing match. And if Caesars can't overcome this in the casino it's written off as an advertising expense, because literally one hundered million people will be watching that fight on TV. And the mention of Caesars Palace, and the pictures of Caesars Palace, is very meaningful. It's also very effective."

What do you suppose is the break-even point at Caesars Palace? How much money does the casino have to win each month to keep its doors open? Caesars Palace, the flagship resort of Caesars World, must roll up a profit of *thirteen million dollars* every 30 days to meet its expenses! Over at the Dunes the monthly nut is $6 million. At the Sands it's $5 million, and even the small (by comparison) Marina Hotel—with 700 rooms—has to win $2.2 million.

There are 50 casinos of note in Las Vegas. Roughly one-third of those are what would be considered major hotel-casino-resorts; the remaining two-thirds are around the size of the Marina, or smaller. So a ballpark figure on the break-even line for all 50 casinos in Las Vegas would have to be somewhere in the neighborhood of $150,000,000 per month! And you thought *you* had a big house payment.

Las Vegas casinos must keep their rooms stocked with plenty of people, each with their $1,000 to spend on gambling. If they don't, the light would blink off one by one and Las Vegas would become just another ghost town out west.

Somehow or other the sky never falls, and the people keep coming, and the profits keep soaring. In 1984 alone, total revenue for the state of Nevada—including rooms, food, beverages and gambling—came to almost $5 billion! That's more than some *countries* bring in. For the Las Vegas Strip the figure was $2,162,793,583; for downtown Las Vegas it was a little over $593 million, with most of the revenue generated through the casinos.

Caesars World alone showed profits for the fiscal year ending July 31, 1985, of $31.8 million, a 69 percent jump over the preceding year's profit of $18.8 million. That includes Caesars in Atlantic City, which reported net gains of $9.7 million all by itself. A lot of that was because of a $90 million expansion program giving the New Jersey casino an added 11,000 square feet of gambling space.

That's quite a figure, considering the original Caesars in Las Vegas cost only $35 million to *build* in 1966.

Of course, Caesars in Vegas isn't the only man-muncher on the prowl. There's the MGM Grand Hotel, one of the biggest dragons in the countryside. Early in 1986 the MGM will have become the Bally Grand; the 26-story hotel, with its 2,832 rooms and suites, was sold in late 1985 to the Bally Corporation for $550 million.*

Bally didn't buy the MGM logo, however, so the famous MGM lion is heading back to Hollywood. Unfortunately, the lion is on just about everything in the hotel, which means replacing ashtrays, drinking glasses, signs, and 175,000 square yards of carpeting, enough to cover 44 football fields! MGM publicist Stephen Allen figures it will cost over a million dollars to do it, or rather, undo it.

The Grand *is* grand, no doubt about it. It's on 43 acres of valuable real estate, and the casino is so big (60,000 square feet) that you could play the Super Bowl in it. The hotel has 4,000 employees and serves more meals in an average day (30,000) than there were *people* in Las Vegas in 1948. Maybe the hotel should call itself the Bally Big Boy, or the Bally-hoo, or even the Bally-High.

The casino has more than 1,000 slot machines, 94 blackjack tables, 10 craps tables, nine roulette wheels, 19 poker

---

*The actual sales price of the Grand Hotel was $440 million. The $550 million figure included $110 million, the amount spent by Kirk Kerkorian as settlement for the 1980 fire at the hotel which claimed 84 lives. The hotel's insurance company has been sued for that amount, and the case is still in litigation.

As tragic as the Grand Hotel fire was, it did cause Las Vegas resorts to completely revamp their fire safety measures. The Grand Hotel alone spent seven million dollars for a complete life safety support system in the unlikely case of another blaze. Other hotels were required to install automatic sprinklers in ceilings, and other safety precautions, all part of what came to be known as "hotel retrofitting."

games, two Big Six wheels and a keno lounge that seats 90 players. The baccarat room is highlighted with Italian marble and crystal chandeliers, hundreds of which droop deliciously throughout the hotel.

If you missed the original sinking of the Titanic in 1912 you can see it go down twice a night in the Grand Hotel's Ziegfeld Room. The show, which cost $10 million to produce, is called "Jubilee," and features close to a hundred showgirls wearing costumes that average 40 pounds each and cost upwards of $5,000 per dress. There are 1,000 costume changes in the show!

The most lavish showroom in Las Vegas is at the Las Vegas Hilton, a two-thousand-seat pleasure palace with sparkling chandeliers (of course) and gold-painted cherubs on a sky-blue ceiling complete with *clouds*. This is where Elvis was king, back in the early seventies. There's a life-sized statue of him next to the showroom, and a display case containing one of his guitars and several of his glittering outfits.

The first song ever sung in the Hilton showroom was by Barbra Streisand when in 1969 the $60 million hotel opened under the name "International." The song, believe it or not, was "I've Got Plenty Of Nothing." She was singing it in a hotel that—at the time—had 1,519 rooms, six restaurants and an 8-acre roof with a putting green on it.

This Y-shaped critter-cruncher was so colossal that its closest rival, Howard Hughes' 476-room Landmark, could fit inside it! The more *people* it lured inside the bigger it got. In 1975 it added an East Tower, in 1978 a North Tower, and in 1979 a North Tower Annex. Known as "the largest resort complex in the entire world," it now is up to 3,174 rooms with more than 3,600 employees. That's almost one for every guest.

As to how much the 375-foot, 30-story hotel is worth
. . . Barron Hilton was once reportedly offered $400
million for it and his answer was, "It's not enough."

The sleekest sapien-swallower on the Strip is the
Tropicana Hotel. It recently spewed up $70 million to add
a 22-story tower which is connected to its other tower by
a glass-enclosed *people mover.* The whole thing looks down
on five acres of waterfalls and tropical plants and what is
billed as the world's largest swimming pool, a quarter of
a mile in diameter.

So here's Las Vegas, with the biggest casino hotel resort
in the world and the largest swimming pool in the world.
The convention capital of the world, it calls itself, and now
the rodeo capital of the world. It's also described, along
with Tokyo and Mexico City, as the *sign* capital of the
world. And it spends millions of dollars, using those neon
billboards, to coax billions of dollars from all those people.

In downtown Glitter Gulch there's the first of the elec-
tric giants, Vegas Vic of the Pioneer Club . . . still tipping
his hat and still gunning for Lee Marvin.

At Circus Circus there's Lucky, a 13-story lighted clown
beckoning the people to stop there.

The Sahara says it's got the biggest sign, 22 stories high
at a cost of a million dollars. Beckoning the people.

Palace Station, located down one of the side roads used
by incoming Californians, says *it's* got the biggest sign.
Publicity Director Leo Diamond boasts that their billboard
is 145 feet high *and* 126 feet wide, "which makes it the
largest in the country that we know of." Cost? Six hundred thousand plus tax.

The Stardust says it's got the brightest sign, and that's
no contest. Forty thousand light bulbs keep the 18-story

sign going. With 30 miles of wiring, 38 tons of steel, paint, and concrete, beckoning the people.

Sam's Town on the Boulder Highway, coming in to Vegas from Arizona-way, spent $700,000 on its outdoor signs. Seven hundred thousand seems like a lot of money, until you think about all those people—each with their thousand dollars to spend on gambling. If that's the case, and it's what the figures say, then Sam's Town only needs 700 of them, and all those signs are paid for!

Plus here's the real kicker. Because of cheap power from nearby Hoover Dam those flashy signs cost hardly anything at all to operate. Would you believe $2,500 a month for the really big ones? In this day and age when the average homeowner's utility bill is over a hundred dollars? Ask U.S. Senator Howard Metzenbaum, who criticized the whole setup in Washington.

The cost wouldn't be important to the casino owners, anyway. They'd pay whatever it costs, and do whatever it takes. They have to, to get the people.

Take Atlantic City. Winter is a four-letter word in New Jersey. Brrr. When tourists there change from bathing suits into wool overcoats the resort's eleven gambling casinos have to come up with quite a few tricks to fill their hotel rooms. The winter months are the worst, so that's when people get the best bargains . . . reduced room rates, a free bottle of bubbly, weekly boxing bouts, drawings for prizes of cash and cars.

"We have to keep those doors turning," says Dennis Gorski of Trump's Castle Hotel and Casino. So Trump's gives away a $50,000 Mercedes Benz.

The Claridge can only come up with a Ford Mustang, but also has a lottery for $50,000 in cash.

The Tropicana plays "Spin to Win" for $100,000.

If you thought Nevada and New Jersey were nip-and-tuck on gambling revenue, guess again. Atlantic City, even with its $2 billion-a-year business in the casinos, is way down in third place, behind Nevada (number one) and California (number two). That's according to an unofficial study done by the Nevada State Gaming Control Board. Stu Curtis of the Board says "it wouldn't surprise me" if the Golden State overtook Nevada because of the "lottery."

Most of the players who come to Las Vegas roll in from California, and that has gaming executives worried. Not because of all the people from California who come, but because of all the people from California who might *quit* coming due to that state's new lottery. It has greatly expanded the public's access to gambling. For example, ten million tickets are sold each day for the California lottery, through 21,000 retail outlets.

The lottery, perhaps more than any other form of gambling, appeals to people's urge to get rich quick. The payoff is high—two million dollars for a $1 ticket—but the odds are even higher. The chances of winning the top prize are 25 million to one, but who cares.

One fellow papered his walls with $2,500 in lottery tickets —not even a one-dollar winner in the bunch. Five California supermarket chains reported that during the first month of selling lottery tickets, grocery sales went *down* five percent.

All in all, Californians were said to have bet more than *ten billion dollars* on gambling in 1985, more than half of it illegally. Of that, $1.5 billion was left in Las Vegas casinos because 67 percent of the tourist trade in southern Nevada comes out of California.

If those people *quit* coming, there will likely be some new names on the Las Vegas Strip. The Dunes will become the Doomed, the Desert Inn will be the Deserted Inn and the Bally Grand will go Bally Up. The Showboat will turn into the Slowboat, and the Castaways will Waste-aways. Down the tumbleweed-strewn boulevard will be the Blandmark, the Maroona, the Las Vegas Tiltin' and the Flopicana.

Las Vegas has been in trouble before. Surely it has another ace or two up its sleeve?

CHAPTER 13

The Crystal Ball

During the 1960's, as the famed Las Vegas "Strip" grew longer and longer, some people contended that "Downtown" Las Vegas had grown bad, like an orange that hangs on a tree too long.

It was a place for people down on their luck, who had just enough money for a fifty-cent shrimp cocktail that was mostly lettuce and glass. Dealers worked there only long enough to polish their trade, and then they fled to the Strip. Why not? The signs along the Strip advertised the good things in life—direct flights to Rome and Rio, a fur sale at Neiman's, a champagne brunch at Caesars. Downtown it was cheap weddings, 24-hour divorces, food fit for a king ("Here King, here boy") and used cars on street corners "For Sale by Owner."

The Strip had all the suitors now, and profits that shot to the moon. 1975—$100 million. 1977—$150 million. 1978—$260 million. 1979—$325 million. 1980—$375 million. Then a nationwide recession, which had ricocheted across the country beginning in 1979, caught up with Las Vegas. Profits began to backslide. "It's only temporary," the Strip casinos exclaimed. The carefully-worded press releases carried terse messages like: "Some casinos are suffering but these were marginal operations in the best of times . . . The strong casinos are holding up . . . We aren't recession-proof but we are recession-resistant.''

Meanwhile, there was another place over on the East Coast that had fallen on hard times before this. It was Atlantic City, New Jersey, once known as "America's Most Popular Resort Destination.'' In 1977 it had 40,000 residents doing battle for just 13,000 jobs. Then, a 1976 referendum that legalized casino gambling began to slowly change all that, and by 1981 almost 20 million people were sticking their big toes in the water at Atlantic City . . . 20 million big toes that Las Vegas needed urgently.

In 1984 almost 29 million people passed up Las Vegas to go to Atlantic City, mostly from throughout the heavily-populated East Coast cities.

"There's no doubt about it, Atlantic City has kicked us in the ass.'' That's the way one Las Vegas gamer put it. "Before Atlantic City came along we had a very unique situation here. If the whole place (Las Vegas) were dragged 40 miles down the road, to the California state line, we'd all be arrested. Gambling was against the law everywhere else. Then Atlantic City jumped on the bandwagon, and for a while Las Vegas almost crumbled.''

The main attraction of Atlantic City was, of course, its location. Over a quarter of the nation's population, some 55 million people, were within one hour's driving distance of the casinos. That meant that wealthy gamblers from the East didn't have to spend four or five hours flying to Las Vegas any longer. Now they could be chauffeured by limousine or helicopter directly to Atlantic City and be back home the same evening.

There were no carefully-worded press releases this time. The Strip was in big trouble. Profits nosedived. 1981—$340 million. 1982—$255 million. 1983—$120 million. It was obvious that Las Vegas would have to change its ways, or else the other slogan it has earned might start being used. "The House Foreclosure Capital of the World." (1,200 in 1985 alone.)

The hotel owners huddled with their department heads, and the public accountants huddled with their computers. The casinos began more aggressive marketing programs, aimed at recapturing the magic that had always given Las Vegas that little edge over everybody else. Conventions were stepped up, along with special events like golf tournaments, professional boxing matches, blackjack tourneys, celebrity poker games, and rodeos. The Frontier Hotel even considered putting a $25,000 casino chip inside a gas-filled balloon and turning it loose, but that gimmick never got off the ground. All of it was a desperate gamble by a desperate city. Las Vegas had already gone through most of the Beaujolais in its wine cellar; now it was time to break out the Ripple. In other words, since there were no longer enough high rollers to go around, the city began to cater to anyone anywhere with any dough they could spare.

Somehow the gamble paid off. 1984—$196 million. 1985—$298 million. Wall Street analysts now predict that this upward trend will continue for the rest of this decade, at around eight percent. It seems that more tourists than ever before are falling for the new Vegas pitch that—coupled with family packages and bargain airfares—sent 14 million of them swarming into the Nevada city in 1985.

Now even Downtown is springing back. This jaded lady, who has been pushed around and shoved around for 40 years by the Strip, has developed its own "master plan," one that was adopted by the City Council in 1984. The three-phase program promises to give Glitter Gulch something she has never had before: a look of sophistication, for want of a better word. By the time her face-lift is complete, she'll be able to sip tea with Ghirardelli Square in San Francisco and not feel like she is from the wrong side of the tracks.

Phase One of this 15-year development plan is already underway. It will feature a shuttle system and another one of those *people*-mover contraptions! This one, though, will be able to transport 5,000 people between the two stations in the downtown area.

Phase Two will focus on nine blocks, or 28 acres, around City Hall downtown. It calls for the development of a civic plaza like most other large U.S. cities have. Phase Three will give downtown its own Fremont Street Mall.

Of course, the casinos downtown are doing their part to keep the "glitter" in Glitter Gulch. Even though Steve Wynn of the Golden Nugget says all that growth is "a little frightening," the president of his hotel complex is optimistic about the future. Bobby Baldwin says, "It's just going to get better and better. Our income—our per-unit win as we call it—is already equal to or exceeds anywhere on the Strip."

Junket business to southern Nevada took on a whole new approach by using one of Atlantic City's own ideas, casino busing. A customer from California, or Arizona, could now travel to Las Vegas in air-conditioned comfort . . . get a free meal . . . and be loaded down with gambling coupons . . . all for a twenty-dollar bill.

Las Vegas stepped up its number of conventions and trade shows, bringing in groups like the National Association of Broadcasters, Shell Oil Company, the National Medical Association, Wendy's Hamburgers, State Farm, and even Alcoholics Anonymous.

If you don't think conventions are big business in Las Vegas now, guess again. Since Atlantic City legalized gambling less than a decade ago there have been 3,211 conventions held in Las Vegas, attended by some five and a half million delegates. The revenue from 1984 alone was over $792 million. The Convention Center has over a million square feet, making it the largest single-level building of its type in the country. There is also an additional million square feet of convention space available in local hotels.

"Conventions definitely help you during the week," one casino boss said. "We'd be hurting without them. On the other side of the coin, it doesn't do us any good as far as the *weekend* business is concerned."

"Besides, there's a big difference between a convention of scrap iron distributors, or beer wholesalers, and someone like the Women Bankers Association, whose members would rather go shopping. It's another story, though, with someone in a high-risk business like scrap iron, or even army surplus. It's a fact that people who gamble in their work will also gamble in their off-hours. These are the ones we're after."

By the year 2000, when McCarran Airport will live up to its new name of McCarran 2000, the population is expected to double in Las Vegas. That means there will be more than one million people to contend with, people with homes and cars and money in their pockets. Thousands come every year to stay, attracted not only by the free-wheeling spirit of Las Vegas, but by industry, sunshine, and wide-open spaces.

What could that do to the gaming industry? Former Tropicana head Robert Harrington thinks it could make the casinos almost self-supporting. "What casinos are here now could probably count on 20 percent of their business by local clientele, which would help them overcome their operating costs and become profitable. Rather than shoot for 100 percent, where the casinos have to get their business from out of town, let's get 80 percent out of town and cultivate the 20 percent that we've got here.''

In order to do this, Harrington thinks there should be a moratorium on new casino construction. The old rule of thumb was "if we build too fast, we're going to be spread out too much. And they held on to that. Then around 1960, a new governor appointed a new (gaming) commission. These people just went wild and let them build all these new hotels. And it started to hurt; the pinch was felt. They were competing against each other . . . giving away this, giving away that, to get the customers to come into their particular hotel. Right now a moratorium should be set in this town, and no more hotels and gaming casinos allowed to open.''

Harrington is right about the sixties. In that short ten-year stretch, eight major resorts flung open their doors in Las Vegas, or one every 15 months: The Castaways, Aladdin, Four Queens, Caesars Palace, Frontier, Circus Circus, Landmark, and the Las Vegas Hilton (International). A moratorium might not be a bad idea. It could help stabilize the gambling economy in Las Vegas, and keep these colossal monsters from devouring one another.

Because, let's face it, the opposition to legalized gambling across America is mellowing. Lotteries proved that. Gross sales for the 21 U.S. lotteries operating in 1985 reached an all-time high of $10.2 billion. Lottery legislation is pending in ten other states, which could mean more than $1.1 billion in government revenues. Las Vegas casino owners plainly don't like the new competition.

"Give me my change in lottery tickets," Californians would say, but then they're born gamblers out there anyway. They have to be to get on those freeways. But listen to this. In 1985 Californians gambled an unprecedented $800 million on their new state lottery, or $30.30 worth of tickets for every man, woman and child in the state, and kids can't play.

Who says the California Gold Rush is over!

This new fantasy is sweeping the state like some gigantic vacuum cleaner, which is exactly what it is. After computerized numbers games are added, lottery experts predict annual sales of two *billion* dollars in California. Not too shabby, especially when the current market value of all that gold mined in the first full year of the original California Gold Rush is just $160 million. The state education system has already made that much, and more, in supplemental funding from the lottery. (The lottery is required to turn over 34 percent of its proceeds to education.)

There always seems to be a follow-up story when somebody in California wins one of those things. Two recent winners, each the recipient of $2 million, were discovered to be illegal aliens from Mexico. They not only got their money, but a little something extra—deportation notices from the U.S. Immigration Service. It was like Johnny Carson said on his TV show: "Everyone in Los Angeles makes two New Year's resolutions. First, to win the lottery, and second, to become an American citizen."

It's not just California where gambling is flourishing, though. Stanley N. Wellborn, Associate Editor of U.S. News And World Report, said in 1980 that at that time—which was well before lotteries even got started—gambling was prospering in 44 American states. He said that 80 percent of this country's citizens approved of gambling in one form or another.

So what happened to New Jersey? The eleven casinos there hauled in a record-breaking $2 billion in 1985, but that didn't mean beans. After salaries and taxes and other expenses were taken out, the profit picture was slightly out of focus . . . somewhere between 60 and 70 million dollars. It's fairly easy to understand why. Each casino's *daily* operating cost is half a million dollars.* And two-thirds of the city's total property tax is paid by the casinos.

Atlantic City casinos *do* get the people, however, something like 30 million a year, as compared with 14 million in Las Vegas. But if they don't want to sleep at the bar, they might have to sleep in their car. Hotel rooms are at a premium—9,000 opposite 60,000 in Vegas. Convention business is limited. Nobody seems to want them. Direct plane flights are limited. The only ones coming in to Atlantic City's Bader Field airport are from New York, Philadelphia and Washington, D.C.

The result of all this is that people spend an average of six hours in Atlantic City, while in Las Vegas they'll stay for three long days. In Las Vegas people can gamble 24 hours a day, but for some weird reason casino hours in Atlantic City practically have to be memorized: 10 a.m. to 4 a.m. on weekdays, and 10 a.m. to 6 a.m. on weekends.

But, oh what a history Atlantic City has had. At first, in the late 1890s, it was a quaint little Victorian resort. Guests were met at the railroad station by horse-drawn carriages, and they would clop-clop past carnival rides and saltwater taffy stands. By the 1920s, there was a bustling Boardwalk, and bathing beauty contests.

*From figures released by Drexel Burnham Lambert Inc., 1986.

By the 1970s Atlantic City had hit the skids. Its citizens started to hit the road. The whole place began to decay, and its only claim to fame any more was that its streets were the names of pieces of property on a Monopoly board.

In 1976, Atlantic City finally got a "get out of jail free" card when New Jersey voters approved the referendum on gambling. Two years later Resorts International opened the first casino in Atlantic City; followed by Caesars Atlantic City, Bally's Park Place, the Sands, Harrah's Marina, the Golden Nugget, the Atlantis, the Claridge, the Tropicana, the Trump Casino Hotel and Trump's Castle. They looked like "eleven Taj Mahals in a war zone," according to one long-time Atlantic City resident. And that was the problem. People were afraid to leave the hotels and go anywhere else. The business district was largely deserted, with soaped-over windows and dingy tenements dotting the countryside. It was nothing like Las Vegas, nothing at all.

Profits in Atlantic City hit an all-time high in 1983 ($168.7 million), beating out Las Vegas for the first and only time. But it's been all downhill ever since. 1984—$121 million, 1985—maybe $70 million. The Atlantis lost $17 million in the first six months of '85 and was forced to file for bankruptcy. Two more hotels are under construction, but neither is expected to open until 1987. That's good, according to analysts, who say the lull will give the existing casinos a chance to regroup. They blame reduced profits on too much competition among the hotels, and an over-saturation of the city's nearby market.

Another thing that has hurt Atlantic City is the lack of communication between the casinos and its tough Casino Control Commission.

One casino vice-president says, "Comparing the Nevada Gaming Control Board to the New Jersey Casino Control

Commission is like comparing the Boy Scouts to the Marines.'' One commission member said in the newspapers that Atlantic City casinos, "even the honest ones,'' catered to pimps, prostitutes, muggers and arsonists. Said another, "We want to control the integrity of this state. Our inspectors are at the casinos 24 hours a day . . . it's a state of mind with these casino guys. They come from Vegas and expect things to be just as loose here.''

Good things are coming Atlantic City's way, if the management firm of Laventhol and Horwath is right. Spokesman Saul Leonard says, "We forecast gross revenues will rise by approximately 10 percent in 1986—to $2.4 billion.'' And: "A step in the right direction is the recently-appointed Atlantic City Reinvestment Authority. There is nothing wrong with Atlantic City that Atlantic City itself and good management cannot cure.''

Maybe. Maybe not. Las Vegas publisher Hank Greenspun wrote in his newspaper column in February of 1986 that "hard reality has diminished the early flush of success that brought euphoria to our sister city on the East Coast. The horizon is no longer bright and beautiful. It's turned to a dull and somewhat despairing gray.''

As for Las Vegas, Greenspun believes that the "corporate policy''—which changed Las Vegas so drastically—is slowly doing an about-face. Vegas isn't entering a new era, he says, but going back to an old one. "When the corporate image came in, they decided they would have to make each department self-supporting.'' But what's the difference whether a person with $500 spends it on a room . . . or on meals . . . or a show? Or if he blows it on the craps table in the casino? "They were going to get the five hundred before he left town, and that's the main thing.'' Consequently, Greenspun said, the casinos "were more hospitable. They comped your room; they comped your show; they comped your drinks. And then that started to disappear.

"Instead of serving food at the shows, you had to buy tickets. It was like going to a movie. And they cut out the drinks (in the showroom) for a while at Caesars Palace. Just see the show, and then get out and get into the casino, or go to one of their restaurants.

"But that philosophy is changing now. They're going back to the old hospitality. And you're going to see more and more of it. Free rooms again, free meals again. I don't know how long it's going to last. It all depends on profitability."

Some people want to roll out legalized gambling in Florida. West Virginia would like to wink at the Constitution. The governor of Louisiana has been a longtime advocate of casinos in his state, and even hopes to someday see gambling ships operating on the Mississippi out of New Orleans. But some of Gov. Edwin Edwards' quotes leave people scratching their heads.

"I am not advocating gambling," he once said. "I am advocating the business of gambling." And another time he said, "There are good reasons for not doing what I propose. There are better reasons for doing it. The good reasons will have to give way to the better ones."

Okay, guv, whatever you say. By the way, what *did* you say?

These three states aren't the only jurisdictions where there are serious examinations of casino gambling. Key officials in Mexico want casinos opened along the northern border of their country. Of course, they want the Americans to run them, and the Americans to play in them, and the Americans to pay taxes on them. For the "right of operation."

The Hilton Hotels Corporation is in the process of opening up two international casinos. One is the LaBelle Creole Hotel on the Caribbean island of St. Martin; and the other is on the Australian Gold Coast at Queensland, where its name will practically take up the whole marquee. "Conrad International Hotel And Jupiters Casino." The Hilton chain includes three blue-chip resorts in Nevada—the Reno Hilton, the Flamingo Hilton in Las Vegas, and the Las Vegas Hilton, which is the largest resort hotel in the world.

What is happening is that the economy is getting so bad in so many different parts of the country that people will jump at anything to turn it all around. Lost revenues have to be replaced somehow, so here come the lotteries. Texas suffers a $1.3 billion budget deficit, and suddenly there is a movement to legalize parimutuel horse racing. Oil prices drop, and Louisiana's governor wants gambling. Unemployment goes up, and West Virginia wants gambling. Mexico has an earthquake, and its leaders want gambling.

As Las Vegas soothsayer Hank Greenspun says, "Any state that flirts with the idea of legalized gambling as an alternative to tax reform and other legitimate sources of revenue is playing a form of Russian roulette . . . It's a sad commentary on total fiscal responsibility as a people if we have to rely on such taxes to sustain government."

You can't blame the other states, though. Not when analysts predict combined revenues for 1986 to surpass *six billion dollars* in Nevada and Atlantic City . . . an increase of about 11 percent over 1985.

So the cards turn, and the dice roll, and the roulette wheel spins. On and on and on. And the prime attraction is not Frank Sinatra, or Wayne Newton, or anybody else. It's *money*. Hit a slot machine and lights flash, bells ring, people crowd around. And for a tiny flash of a moment you're the star.

For the bored, it's excitement. For the lonely, it's a mistress.

But for those behind the tables there is no glamour . . . just hard work, and days that flicker into nights. And knowing that tomorrow it's got to be done all over again.

Bibliography

Gambling And The Law, I. Nelson Rose, Gambling Times Inc. 1018 N. Cole, Hollywood, California.

Pay The Line, John Gollehon, Gollehon Press, Inc., Grand Rapids, Michigan, 1985.

U.S.A. Today, Selected Articles, 1986.

All About Blackjack, John Gollehon, Gollehon Press, Inc., Grand Rapids, Michigan, 1985.

Fact Sheet, Atlantic City Casino Assoc., 1985.

Big Julie Of Vegas, Edward Linn, Walker And Co., New York, New York, 1967.

Las Vegas Chamber Of Commerce, 1985.

Fools Of Fortune, John Philip Quinn, G. L. Howe And Co., Chicago, Ill., 1890.

The History Of Gambling In England, John Ashton, Patterson Smith, Montclair, N.J., 1969.

The Gaming Table: Its Votaries And Victims, Andrew Steinmetz, Patterson Smith, Montclair, N.J., 1969.

Play The Devil, Henry Chafetz, Bonan Books, New York, New York, 1960.

Your Best Bet, Mike Goodman, Ballantine books, New York, New York, 1977.

Mr. Lucky, Zack Soderberg, Seven Magazine, Los Angeles, Calif., Sept-Oct., 1985.

Silver Turns To Gold, Stuart Curits, Gaming Control Board, 1981.

Las Vegas News Bureau, 1985.

The Green Felt Jungle, Ed Reid/Ovid Demaris, Trident Press, New York, New York, 1963.

Las Vegas *SUN* Newspaper, selected articles, 1985/86.

Grand Rapids *PRESS,* 1985.

Las Vegas Is My Beat, Ralph Pearl, Citadel Press, Secaucus, N.J., 1978.

Las Vegas *REVIEW-JOURNAL,* selected articles, 1985/86.

Gambling Related Data, Continuous Nat'l Survey of the National Opinion Research Center, Chicago, Feb. 10, 1974.

Legalized Gambling in the United States: A Survey, Congressional Research Service, Library Of Congress, Washington, D.C., August, 1971.

Gambling, Hazard and Reward, O. Newman, Athlone, London, 1961.

A Study Of The Numbers Game in New York City, conducted by Oliver Quayle And Co., Bronxville, N.Y. for the Fund for the City of New York, 1972.

The One-Minute Manager, Jeffrey Silver, Las Vegan Magazine, April, 1985.

Marketing Bulletin, Las Vegas Convention & Visitors Authority, March 15, 1985.

State Of Nevada Regulations: Nevada Gaming Commission and State Gaming Control Board, Carson City, Nevada, 1985.

Las Vegas Visitor Profile Study, Las Vegas Convention & Visitors Authority, 1984.

Corporate Profile, Casino Gaming Magazine, Rockville, Maryland, October, 1985.

Liquid Assets, Seven Magazine, Los Angeles, California, July-Aug., 1985.

Headliners, Las Vegas Magazine, Las Vegas, Nev., Charter Issue, 1985.

Imperial Beach, California *STAR-NEWS,* 1985.

Carole Lombard: The Mystery Of Her Death, Bob Stoldal, LV Magazine, Las Vegas, Nevada, December, 1985.

Superstitions, Mark Christensen, Seven Magazine, 1801 Century Park East, Los Angeles, Calif., July/Aug., 1985.

San Diego *UNION,* 1985.

Casino Gaming, Rockville, Maryland, 1985.

Neon, Tom Wolfe, Seven Magazine, 1801 Century Park East, Los Angeles, Calif., May/June, 1985.

Robert Blade, Florida *TIMES-UNION,* Jacksonville, Florida, Jan. 5, 1986.

All About Roulette, John Gollehon, Gollehon Press, Inc., Grand Rapids, Michigan, 1985.

All About Keno, John Gollehon, Gollehon Press, Inc., Grand Rapids, Michigan, 1985.

All About Craps, John Gollehon, Gollehon Press, Inc., Grand Rapids, Michigan, 1985.

Bud Jones Co., Las Vegas, Nevada. (Dice Specs)

Playing Games For Fun And Profit, Len Miller, Gambling Times, Inc., Hollywood, Calif., 1983.

Winners, Deborah Munch, Seven Magazine, March/April, 1985.

All About Slots And Video Poker, John Gollehon, Gollehon Press, Inc., Grand Rapids, Michigan, 1985.

All About Baccarat, John Gollehon, Gollehon Pres, Inc., Grand Rapids, Michigan, 1985.

The Book Of Lists, Wallechinsky, Wallace & Wallace, Bantam Books, 666 Fifth Ave., New York, New York, 1978.

Las Angeles *HERALD EXAMINER*, 1986.

Las Vegas Visitors Atlas, Red McIlvane, TMA Inc., Las Vegas, Nevada, 1982.

The Lady Of Glitter Gulch, Kimberly Coy, LV Magazine, 2381 A Renaissance Dr., Las Vegas, Nev., Dec., 1985.

The Saga Of Glitter Gulch, Kimberly Coy & Bob Palm, (Part 2) Las Vegas *SUN,* Oct. 28, 1985.

New York, New York, John McLaughlin, Newhouse News Service, Jan. 29, 1986.

People Of Chance, John M. Findlay, Oxford Univ. Press, 1986.

The Los Angeles *TIMES,* selected articles, 1985/86.

World Wide Casino Exchange Newsletter, Star Time, Inc., Las Vegas, Nev.